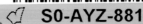

PRESCHOOLERS AND SUBSTANCE ABUSE: STRATEGIES FOR PREVENTION AND INTERVENTION

Pedro J. Lecca, PhD
Thomas D. Watts, DSW

SOME ADVANCE REVIEWS

"Examines an important issue for the first time in a comprehensive manner. Children of substance abusers are poorly served by society and their own parents and merit far more attention than they get now. This book brings together the relevant research on the issues in an interesting and provocative way. It also makes a large number of important recommendations for better programming and policies for children of substance abusers. This book will be of help to anyone interested in the topic."

Reginald G. Smart, PhD, Head, Social Epidemiology, Addiction Research Foundation, Toronto

---

Preschoolers
and Substance Abuse
Strategies for Prevention
and Intervention

HAWORTH Addictions Treatment
F. Bruce Carruth, PhD
Senior Editor

New, Recent, and Forthcoming Titles:

Group Psychotherapy with Addicted Populations by Philip J. Flores

Shame, Guilt and Alcoholism: Treatment Issues in Clinical Practice by Ronald T. Potter-Efron

Neuro-Linguistic Programming in Alcoholism Treatment edited by Chelly M. Sterman

Cocaine Solutions: Help for Cocaine Abusers and Their Families by Jennifer Rice-Licare and Katherine Delaney-McLoughlin

Preschoolers and Substance Abuse: Strategies for Prevention and Intervention by Pedro J. Lecca and Thomas D. Watts

Chemical Dependency and Antisocial Personality Disorder: Psychotherapy and Assessment Strategies by Gary G. Forrest

Substance Abuse and Physical Disability edited by Allen W. Heinemann

Addiction in Human Development: Developmental Perspectives on Addiction and Recovery by Jacqueline Wallen

Preschoolers and Substance Abuse
Strategies for Prevention and Intervention

Pedro J. Lecca, PhD
Thomas D. Watts, DSW

The Haworth Press
New York • London • Norwood (Australia)

The Haworth Press, Inc., 10 Alice Street, Binghamton, NY 13904-1580

Library of Congress Cataloging-in-Publication Data

Lecca, Pedro J., 1936-
  Preschoolers and substance abuse : strategies for prevention and intervention / Pedro J. Lecca, Thomas D. Watts.
      p.   cm.
  Includes bibliographical references and index.
  ISBN 1-56024-235-3 (alk. paper).
      1. Preschool children — United States — Drug use. 2. Drug abuse — United States — Prevention. I. Watts, Thomas D. II. Title.
HV5824.C45L43   1992
372.3'7 – dc20   91-35921
                                                                            CIP

To those who are concerned, recognize the problems, and confront the challenge of substance abuse with families of preschool children.

P.J.L

To Ilene, Rebecca, and Jeanine Watts, and to Ms. Elenora A. Lane and Mr. Paul J. Pruchnicki.

T.D.W.

ABOUT THE AUTHORS

Pedro J. Lecca, PhD, is on the faculty of The University of Texas at Arlington. Dr. Lecca has been interested in the impact of drug abuse on minority groups for a number of years. With over twenty years of experience in drug and drug-related areas pertaining to substance abuse, he has written extensively on the topic and is nationally known for his research and writings. He is a member of the American Public Health Association, the American Pharmaceutical Association, and the Council of Social Work Education.

Thomas D. Watts, DSW, is on the faculty of The University of Texas at Arlington. He has published or co-published a number of books and articles on social welfare, substance abuse, and related areas, including *The World of Social Welfare; Alcohol Problems of Minority Youth in America; Alcoholism in Minority Populations; Native American Youth and Alcohol;* and *Pathways for Minorities into the Health Professions.* Dr. Watts, has served on the Board of Directors of the American Indian Center Rehabilitation Program in Grand Prairie, Texas since 1986.

CONTENTS

Foreword

The "War on Drugs" failed before the first shot was fired. The answer is not in the jungles of Colombia, but in our own neighborhoods. As long as there is demand, human greed will guarantee a supply—if not of cocaine, then of synthetics (which I prefer not to call designer drugs lest we conjure up images of designer jeans) that can be made in any bathtub.

Combatting addiction *after* it has developed is infinitely harder than stopping it *before* it gets started. And that means strategies which affect preschool children. Five-year-olds know that daddy only drinks Old Crow, or that it is gin and not 7-Up that mother drinks when she is ironing. Research shows that attitudes about alcohol and other drugs are already formed by junior high school level, and senior high school is definitely too late.

That is why this book is important. Not that it has magic answers or the perfect solution. But at least it explores the problem from the right perspective, exposes our ignorance and need of research, and points to specific areas where improvement is possible right now with practical suggestions. This includes the statistically important but much neglected populations of Native American Indians, Hispanics, and blacks. The opinions here are not from bureaucrats but from those who live and work with these minority groups.

Recent years of judging the annual Meritorious Award applications for Prevention programs by local affiliates of the National Council on Alcoholism and Drug Dependence (NCADD) have impressed me with their tremendously imaginative and broad prevention efforts which involve the whole community: teachers, parents, police, news media, churches, business—everybody. The book confirms the importance of this by pointing out that prevention must take place in a community and societal context.

One salient point is the degree to which alcohol, our number one drug of abuse, is neglected in both research and social programs. Crack cocaine and heroin might seem more glamorous, but except for good research on the fetal alcohol syndrome, the drug alcohol tends to be ignored, by both the federal government and the news media.

The authors alert us all to the erroneous assumptions behind many research and prevention programs. Issues needing discussion here would include minimizing the role of television (both ads and programs) in forming the ideas and attitudes of even very young children, or the difference between cognitive and other developmental factors at various stages in childhood. I might add the fact that advocating low-risk behaviors has no appeal for adolescents who *love* risk-taking!

Prevention is much more possible than the pessimists think. The failure of scare tactics and prohibition have blinded us to the effectiveness of a health education approach which is positive and factual. There are over 40 million ex-smokers in the United States today, and 90 percent of Americans are drinking less than they did five years ago. Thanks to the efforts of MADD and others, death by a drinking driver is no longer a socially acceptable form of homicide. Critics forget that measuring prevention means measuring a non-event, what did not happen. Also, that primary prevention takes time: e.g., two centuries for Jenner's discovery of vaccination to result in the near-extinction of smallpox. But progress is being made. This book should stimulate more.

James E. Royce, SJ, PhD
Seattle University

Acknowledgements

We are grateful to Julien Devereux, graduate research assistant, who labored diligently on this volume, and to Mary Smith, who typed and helped with the editing of the manuscript. We want to thank the Health Resources and Services Administration, Bureau of Maternal and Child Health and Resources Development, Rockville, MD, for its confidence and support [Contract No. HRSA 89-485(P)]. The views expressed herein are those of the authors. Statements made in this publication do not necessarily represent the views or policies of the funding source.

Serious concern for the problem of addiction, and full awareness of the tremendous impact it has on our everyday lives, means that we must be prepared to accept the inevitable need for fundamental and courageous political and social changes.

—Carl M. Stroh, *Addiction, Society and Self*. Vancouver, British Columbia, Canada: Province of British Columbia Alcohol and Drug Commission, 1980, p. 206.

There is no quick fix for a family system that is dysfunctional in varied and complex ways, delusional, with no good role models, and in a self-perpetuating, unconscious denial. The children have learned all too well the three rules described by Claudia Black: *Don't Tell, Don't Trust, Don't Feel*.

—James E. Royce, SJ, *Alcohol Problems and Alcoholism: A Comprehensive Survey*. Revised Edition. New York: The Free Press, Div. of Macmillan, Inc., 1989, p. 164.

Chapter I

Introduction

This issue is not easy to research or write about. While there is growing research on children of alcoholics and on substance abusers in general, little research exists on substance abuse among families of preschool children. Preschool children are uniquely dependent in almost every respect on their parents. If one or both parents is a substance abuser, then the problem is immense for all concerned. It is possible that teen-age sons or daughters of substance abusing parents could manage to cope in some way, even to move to the home of a relative or friend. Preschool children, on the other hand, are totally dependent on their parents. We do not see many runaway preschoolers, but we do see many runaway teens. To "run away" is a fiercely independent action. Preschool children are not old enough to cope with even thinking about such exigencies. They are rooted in one place, their parents' home, and dependent on them for emotional nurturance, physical support—support of all kinds.

Our discussion of prevention and intervention strategies includes no magic elixirs, nor do the studies that we examined contain instant solutions. Indeed, "even the best of studies have limitations that confound interpretation of the results" (Battjes and Bell, 1985). The complexity of the problem dwarfs the efforts of researchers and writers attempting to make sense of it. Hence, we have no pretensions that solutions will be easily seen or implemented. Substance abuse is so deeply interwoven into U.S. and other societies, that long-term solutions will be difficult, badly needed—but at the same time attainable.

Several years ago six babies in Washington, DC, were abandoned after being born to mothers addicted to crack, a particularly dangerous form of cocaine. Hospital officials say boarder babies such as these at Howard University Hospital are taking up space that could be used for treating older children. While the material cost for dealing with these children is high, from $750 to $1,768 a day (*Fort Worth Star Telegram*, July 2, 1989), the physical and psychological price is immeasurable.

Statistics gathered by the House Select Committee on Children, Youth, and Families suggest that 375,000 newborns a year may be harmed by drug exposure and that last year 11 percent of pregnant women used drugs (*Fort Worth Star Telegram*, July 2, 1989). Although hospital officials say the number of boarder babies is growing, the problem is so recent that nationwide statistics are not available. There is not even a standard definition for boarder babies.

Poverty and deprivation are not the only contributing factors in substance abuse, but they are nevertheless seminal factors that too often have been ignored. Many low-income people seek a "way out" of their situation. Substance abuse often is this way out. Unfortunately, services to low-income substance abusers are sparse, and the ones that are present are sometimes inadequate. With no national health program in place, many low-income substance abusers are left out of the picture. Particularly affected are many of the "working poor," who are ineligible for many health (and other) programs.

The United States "is the only major industrialized nation in the world that does not have a plan or system for delivery of health care. Consequently, we provide less health care coverage to our population than any other major industrialized nation in the world. In addition, we are paying more for our health care than most other nations" (U.S. House of Representatives, 1984). The ones most affected are poor families and poor children. The Children's Defense Fund (1988) states:

- More than 35 million Americans — a third of them are children — lack any type of health insurance, public or private, and are one catastrophic illness away from financial disaster.
- The United States has fallen to a tie for last place among 20 industrialized nations in preventing its babies from dying in the first year of life. . . . Prenatal care utilization by poor

mothers — which can reduce low-birthweight births, birth defects, and infant mortality — is eroding.

• The number of working families without private health insurance has been growing rapidly, and most public health programs are overburdened and underfunded.

• Children are at particular risk. One in three uninsured Americans is a child, and the majority of these children are from low-income families that cannot afford care without insurance.

Poor, substance-abusing parents of preschool children are more likely to be uninsured and hence unable to afford expensive substance abuse treatment. Also, treatment for this population may be even more expensive because of the need for child care.

According to the National Institute on Drug Abuse (1986), 2.5 million adolescents 12 to 17 years old were using marijuana and hashish regularly and 7 million were using alcohol regularly. Often these children live in an environment where there is a family history of substance abuse. It is estimated that 7 million children below the age of 18 live in homes with active alcoholism (National Institute on Alcohol Abuse and Alcoholism, 1987).

Children of substance abusers continue to be the most underserved population in the continuum of care in the recovery field. Most treatment centers do not include these children in family programs, most therapists are not qualified to counsel the total family, and schools do not have community approaches to prevention (Naiditch, 1986).

Marijuana is among the most widely used psychoactive substances in the Western world, although in the United States its use has declined somewhat in recent years. "The decline for young adults (18 to 25) was from 64.1 percent in 1982 to 60.5 percent in 1985. Nevertheless, a total of 18 million Americans used marijuana in the past 30 days; 2.7 million were 12 to 17 years old, 7.1 million were 18 to 25 years old, and 8.4 million were 26 years old or over" (National Institute on Drug Abuse, 1987; U.S. Department of Health, Education and Welfare, 1980). Considerable marijuana use also appears to be occurring among pregnant women, with serious health consequences to themselves and their offspring (Sokol et al.,

1980; Hingson et al., 1982; Linn et al., 1983; Fried et al., 1984; Gibson et al., 1983). It is only in the last few years, however, that critical attention has been focused on the possibility that these substances can cause birth defects and postnatal behavioral aberrations. The National Institute on Drug Abuse (1987) states:

> Drug abuse (with the exception of alcohol abuse) became uncommon following the passage of the Harrison Narcotic Act of 1914. However, during the past twenty years it has emerged as a dominant public health and social concern. In 1960 less than 7 percent of college-age young adults had ever used marijuana; by 1982, a majority (64 percent) of young adults 18-25, nearly two out of three, had done so. Cocaine use for most of this century was restricted to a tiny population. But by 1985, more than one in six (17.3 percent) high school seniors had tried cocaine; nearly a third of our young adults had done so.

Fetal alcohol syndrome has been widely researched and mentioned in the literature, and alcohol remains the most widely used drug among American youth. The early age of first use appears to be the best demographic predictor of alcohol and other drug abuse. Further, alcohol appears to be a gateway leading to other drug use (U.S. Department of Health and Human Services, 1987).

Methadone maintenance has been the heroin addiction treatment of choice for several years. The prenatal and early neonatal effects of methadone have been described in several reports (Kandall et al., 1979; Finnegan, 1983). However, there have been few reports on the long-term effects of methadone maintenance during pregnancy on the child's somatic and neurobehavioral development. Some investigators have described mild neurobehavioral abnormalities, while others have found none (Finnegan, 1983; Wilson et al., 1981; Lifschitz et al., 1983).

The number of women using and abusing non-narcotic drugs exceeds the number addicted to narcotics (Chambers and Hart, 1977). Current data show that 63 percent to 93.5 percent of women use analgesics during pregnancy and that sedative drug use ranges from 22 percent to 28 percent (Doering and Stewart, 1978; Forfar and Nelson, 1973; Hill, 1973).

Public concern over substance abuse in families with preschool children has stimulated a major effort to identify effective ways of deterring onset of this behavior. Traditional health education approaches have proven largely unsuccessful. New approaches, strategies, and interventions hopefully will provide insight and avenues for programs to meet this challenge.

CURRENT IMPACT OF SUBSTANCE ABUSE ON FAMILIES OF PRESCHOOL CHILDREN AND MODELS

In examining the impact of substance abuse on families of preschool children, one encounters a variety of issues that will require diverse, creative, and persistent effort to impact. These range from the relatively clear-cut prevention efforts directed to fetal alcohol syndrome — the mother abstaining from alcohol and other unnecessary drugs during pregnancy (NIAAA, 1987) — to the elusive issue of preventing intergenerational transmission of alcoholism and the spread of substance abuse, which would include treatment of the active alcoholic or substance abuser as well as working with all family members to prevent future problems (Kenward and Rissover, 1980).

The changing drug abuse pattern in society has caused researchers to move prevention efforts to preadolescents (Greenspan, 1985), to accept adolescent drug use as normative statistically (Baumrind, 1985), and to realize that a distinction must be made between use, abuse, and addiction. These adolescents often report being introduced to drugs by a parent or older sibling (Bush and Iannotti, 1985), which implies the significant role played by the family in the onset of drug use.

Federal policy has focused on reducing the supply of illicit drugs through border control, confiscation, and arrest, but it is obvious to anyone who reads a newspaper that this approach is at best ineffective and at worst criminalizes a large segment of the population. This shortsighted, narrow, legalistic focus has been accompanied by a prevention campaign using "scare tactics" that utilized questionable data to support its case and actually may have worsened the problem (Lindesmith, 1982).

The complexity of these issues insists that they be investigated in the context in which they occur and that prevention and intervention must take place in the same context. Certain social problems in the community often are investigated as correlated with substance abuse, and most researchers generally accept that the family has a role in initiating, maintaining, and perpetuating a substance abuse problem (Adler and Raphael, 1983). The debate concerns which social and family problems create substance abuse and vice versa.

These substance abuse problems will be viewed here in the context of the community and the family, and the broader term "substance abuse" will be used to subsume other categories including drug abuse, alcoholism, alcohol abuse, chemical dependency, and addiction. Other terms will be used regarding particular research or programs when they are specified. The intent of this book will be to:

1. briefly state the nature of the substance abuse problem identified by the literature as it affects the child and the family system,
2. discuss the social problems (e.g., violence, crime, sexual abuse, FAS, etc.) often correlated with familial substance abuse,
3. review and analyze the effectiveness of demonstration programs mentioned in the literature on familial substance abuse and related problems, and
4. make policy and research recommendations for future advances and understanding of this important issue.

Although no definitive pattern of deficits, traits, or interactions has emerged that explains the intergenerational transmission of alcoholism or the spread of substance abuse in families, prevention and intervention strategies have been pursued with whatever theoretical foundation was current at the time. Bacon (1987) takes a historical view and suggests that everything done in the past 200 years has been ineffective and plagued by factional beliefs that have hindered progress. He calls for a "common sense" approach.

"Common sense" dictates that some basic questions must be answered before proceeding. What are we trying to prevent? Who or what is the target of this effort? What is the difference between prevention and intervention? To oversimplify the answers, attempts are made to prevent the spread of alcoholism and substance abuse within families and communities and the secondary negative effects such as fetal alcohol syndrome, minimal brain dysfunction, and emotional and behavioral problems in children of substance abusers.

Primary prevention provides information or services that promote healthy attitudes and reduce the occurrence of substance abuse. Secondary prevention, or early intervention, identifies and intervenes with high-risk individuals exhibiting early warning signs before they experience additional problems. Tertiary prevention is intervention with those who are already experiencing problems (Swett, 1984). In the case of alcoholism and drug abuse, this can be considered prevention due to its prevalence in the community and the unexplained transmission of substance abuse and other problems to family members. Moos and Billings (1982) showed that children with alcoholic fathers who had recovered were less depressed and anxious than those whose alcoholic fathers had relapsed and were hospitalized. This implies that the recovery of one family member may reduce risk factors in other members.

What prevention methods will we use? This question will be answered for each problem area discussed. Why do we think that a particular program will work? The answer will be to identify the theoretical perspective or to cite significant findings in those programs with strong evaluations in place.

Most prevention program designs emphasize empowering the individual, the family, and/or the community in order to have a long-lasting impact on any public health problem whether it be targeted toward minorities (Mason and Baker, 1978), low-income communities (Resnick, 1980), adolescents, or families (Ellis, 1980).

A panel convened by the National Institute of Drug Abuse's Office of Program Development and Analysis in June 1978 (Ellis, 1980) was assigned to develop models of practice for family-centered primary prevention that can be demonstrated and evaluated. The results were conceptualized into three models:

1. Ecological Systems or Systems Linkage Model. This model suggests that the vertical organization of many agencies can contribute to dysfunction and suggests a broad goal should be the realignment of societal units in which groups of individuals called families link with groups of families called communities or neighborhoods, which then link with organizations that help individuals, families, and communities. The model would emphasize process and context in a horizontal interactive network rather than a from-the-top-down approach. The task would be to create new links in the community and then step back to monitor and evaluate. This has been described by Bartunek (1982) as a "minimal intervention designed to generate structural systemic change."

2. Family Intervention Model. This model attempts to empower the family's sense of competency and reduce the sense of isolation by providing skills training with psychodynamic group techniques in informal family groups. The emphasis again is the return to traditional family networks developed within these groups to provide the sense of community and social support that has rapidly and spontaneously disappeared in the current culture. The agency role is to facilitate this process rather than to control interaction or provide a service delivery model of treatment.

3. Media Model. The last model addresses the unrealistic image of the family as presented on television and advertising and the power that the media have to change attitudes and opinions. The strategy is to provide models of functional families and how they cope and seek support within the family and community. This could be done through public service announcements and cable television and network entertainment shows that represent family life. There were no strategies discussed to achieve this model or how to motivate those with decision-making power to commit to it (Ellis, 1980).

These models compare current strategies with what was considered effective based on prevention research at the time and to reflect the change in emphasis from treating the individual to realigning the community, the helping agency, and the family in order to help the individual not use drugs or alcohol in a health-compromising way. It is this focus on changing social norms, strengthening the family, and making agencies more responsive to needs that differentiates prevention from intervention.

COMMUNITY PERSPECTIVES

America has become a chemically dependent society that offers its children mixed messages regarding the use of mood-changing chemicals. We have "bad drugs" (heroin, cocaine) and "bad users" (alcoholics, addicts). Some drugs like opiates are "bad" on the street but "good" if prescribed by a doctor (Swett, 1984). Other drugs like tobacco are considered "bad" but are sold in machines on the street. The trends in social thought about alcohol have been traced by Watts (1982) as the

1. moral perspective that views alcohol as evil and those who drink it as weak-willed;
2. the disease concept that views alcohol as neutral and those who drink it to excess as sick with a disease called alcoholism;
3. the new public health view that alcohol is not entirely neutral, that availability has social consequences and that social control and reduction of overall consumption are worthwhile goals.

All three of these perspectives and others exist today in varying degrees in religious, social, and ethnic communities. The result: contradictory social policy. The Supreme Court decision (*McKelvey v. Turnage*, 1988) ruling in favor of the Veterans Administration used a moralistic view of alcoholism to deny benefits to many veterans, and yet the Hughes Act of 1970 institutionalizes the disease concept in most other federal arenas. From a social perspective, youth use drugs because they lack guidance and clear direction from the society they live in regarding their own chemical health.

In a panel discussion regarding the intersection of violence, crime, sexual abuse, and addiction, Dr. Densen-Gerber (Panel Workshop . . . , 1976) made the provocative statement that "being born within a nuclear family is the first act of violence we inflict upon our young." She further explains her view that the "nuclear family'' was created by modern industry because its members could move easier than could an extended family. She emphatically states that man is a ''herd'' animal and needs the additional support of a rooted, extended family. She mentions common goals, common commitment, common values, common sense of custom, and a common direction as the roots necessary for supporting the nuclear family. This context could be called community or neighborhood as well as extended family and calls for the type of response suggested by the Systems Linkage Model of responsive communities and agencies to solve family problems.

Chapter II

Prenatal and Postnatal Consequences of Maternal Substance Abuse

The most fundamental form of family is a woman and her child. Little research exists on the impact of maternal drug addiction and alcoholism on a child's development, as most studies have focused on male children of male alcoholics in order to isolate the biogenetic transmission mechanism that appears more pronounced in male alcoholics and in children of alcoholic fathers (McKenna and Pickens, 1981). Bepko (1988) discusses how the cultural male/female roles have different significance for a family with a substance-abusing father or mother and how they require different treatments. She also suggests that the dominance or power issues in a family often reflect an individual's socialization as a male or female. The research done on maternal substance abuse has been in the area of prenatal and perinatal effects on the child, and since the ability to get pregnant is exclusively female this is a beginning in understanding the complex motives in female substance abuse and how to prevent and treat it. With the dissolution of the Soviet Union, reports from health officials are indicating the impact that alcohol and other drugs are having on mothers and their children.

The estimated incidence of full, developed fetal alcohol syndrome (FAS) is one to three per 1,000 births, averaged from reports from Sweden, France, and the United States, with milder cases estimated to be one in 300 (Landesman-Dwyer, 1982). If this indicator holds, then FAS would be the most preventable form of mental retardation and birth defects (NIAAA, 1987). No reported cases of fully developed FAS have been found except in children born to mothers identified as chronic alcoholics. This phenomenon is not dose-specific to alcohol. The detrimental effects on the child are on a continuum from smaller head diameter and lower birth weight in children of women who report moderate drinking to severe soft tissue malformation and damage to the central nervous system in fully developed FAS. These more subtle developmental defects have been termed fetal alcohol effects (FAE) and alcohol-related birth defects (ARBD) and are characterized as developmental delays or minimal brain dysfunction (Landesman-Dwyer, 1982). There are intervening variables such as nutrition, smoking, and the mother's weight, but most of the risk can be avoided by the mother abstaining from alcohol and other unnecessary drugs during pregnancy. Some physical anomalies characteristic of FAS would indicate that the damage occurs in the first trimester but birth weight is achieved in the final trimester (Landesman-Dwyer, 1982). This indicates damage to the fetus throughout the pregnancy.

The challenge is how to disseminate this information to all women of child-bearing age in a manner that will change their drinking behavior (primary), how to counsel and treat those who now have an alcohol problem and are unable to stop on their own (secondary), and finally how to intervene with pregnant women who have a drinking problem (tertiary) and women who already have had a child who exhibits FAS characteristics.

The specific target population profile are women between ages 18 and 34. The National Institute on Alcohol Abuse and Alcoholism's 1982 campaign estimated that 22 percent of all women 18-34 heard public service announcements about drinking while pregnant. This campaign was carried out by state and local governments, volunteers, and the March of Dimes (NIAAA, 1987). Increasing the awareness of risks has often had a boomerang effect in drug abuse prevention programs and there is no data to support the perspective that disseminating knowledge alone is effective in changing attitudes and behavior (Kinder et al., 1980).

A comprehensive program implemented at the community level was most effective in raising the general awareness of drinking and pregnancy in the Pregnancy Health Project conducted by the University of Washington between 1978 and 1981 (NIAAA, 1987). The strategy was to impact the attitudes of those who might influence the drinking choices of the targeted women, including spouses, parents, and friends. The program also provided printed material, counseling aimed at the target population, and training for health care professionals on the risks of drinking and pregnancy. This program included components of all three models mentioned previously and had strategies aimed at the first and second levels of prevention.

A more specific profile of high-risk women emerged in an analysis of data (Landesman-Dwyer, 1982) from numerous large sample studies. The characteristics identified were consistent. Women who drink heavily tend to be older, to have had more pregnancies, to be of lower socioeconomic status, to weigh more, to receive less prenatal care, and to smoke and use other drugs more. High-risk women include single women with children and those who are looking for work. By definition these women would likely be in a lower socioeconomic situation than married women who are employed and have no children. Some consideration for programs that target low SES women (NIAAA, 1987):

1. The cognitive and educational level of the client.
2. Low SES women do not necessarily link their behavior to the health of their babies.
3. Information can be disseminated to women awaiting care at public health clinics due to their accessibility and health motivation.
4. Women with more education are more likely to alter their behavior after educating themselves about risk factors than women with a high school education or less.
5. "Scare tactics" that invoke guilt in the mothers may increase drinking and should be avoided. Positive messages promoting health are more effective.
6. Methods in order of effectiveness for this population include:
   a. individual counseling
   b. education classes
   c. audio-visual material
   d. printed material.

Also included in this high-risk group are victims of rape or incest and women with alcoholic husbands or alcoholic mothers (NIAAA,

1987). This profile parallels the characteristics reported by Black, Bucky and Wilder-Padilla (1986) of adult children of alcoholics.

The age of onset for drinking and smoking in women is decreasing by as much as two years in one study (Clayton et al., 1986). This factor combined with the current high incidence of teen-age pregnancy points to an urgent need for primary prevention messages and health programs beginning in the elementary grades.

More black women abstain from alcohol, but those who drink, drink heavily (NIAAA, 1987). Inner city minorities should be targeted and researched as individual groups to gain maximum data significance and to respect cultural differences. Women of color are at higher risk for FAS than white women. Other considerations for minorities include incomplete acculturation, powerlessness, language barriers, discrimination, and lack of insurance coverage for treatment (Resnick, 1980). Religious and cultural differences in viewing alcoholism and addiction also can prevent women, especially Hispanic and Native American women, from seeking treatment.

At especially high risk are Native American women of the Southwest. The Plains groups have the highest rate of alcoholism, which is exacerbated by the cultural demand that women remain abstinent. Those women who do not or cannot are ostracized and end up living on the fringes of society. In a study by May (1982) the incidence of FAS in children born to these women was 1.3 per mother. Fortunately, this number is highly concentrated, illustrated by the statistic that all FAS children in this group are born to six out of 1,000 women. Jeaneen Grey Eagle, who directs an alcohol treatment program at the Pine Ridge reservation in South Dakota, says the problem was so serious that it was "threatening the very survival of the Indian people" (Kolata, 1989).

The U.S. Indian Health Service created the National Indian Fetal Alcohol Syndrome Prevention Program in 1983 to deliver prevention training services and materials to tribal groups with a primary focus on equipping more trainers. This is strictly primary prevention but culturally sensitive to the target population.

In a prenatal clinic in Boston City Hospital, a tertiary prevention (early intervention) program between 1974 and 1979 demonstrated that heavy drinkers could be treated for alcohol problems while pregnant with a significant decrease in growth retardation and congenital defects in their babies (NIAAA, 1987).

In the same hospital, the classification of compatible with fetal alcohol syndrome (CFAS) was used to identify subjects who exhibited some but not all of the FAS criteria. Women who smoked marijuana were five times more likely to give birth to a child with CFAS deficiencies than women with no drug use (Zuckerman, 1985). Tennes, Avitable, Blackard, Boyles, Hassoun, Holmes and Kreye (1985) refuted this finding on the grounds that it did not account for the fact that women who smoke marijuana fit a high-risk profile in other categories.

Zuckerman (1985) suggests that other drugs may affect placental development and that alcohol is consumed in greater quantities and by more women than other substances, which explains the association of alcohol with certain defects. Other characteristics associated with CFAS mothers are similar to FAS, e.g., low SES, heavy smoking, and drinking. This suggests that all variables have not been noted in the research to make this syndrome substance-specific.

One explanation for the variance is the fact that most research relies on drug use self-report by the mother. High-risk women may tend to report socially desirable answers regarding specific drugs or levels of use and not report others. In one study, eight of 18 women reported not using any marijuana during the test period but showed positive for marijuana metabolites in their urinalysis. Unverified self-report data could lead researchers to attribute effects to the wrong substance (Zuckerman, 1985).

Other studies have indicated that alcohol and other drugs, i.e., opiates, alcohol, and cocaine, have either direct impact on the developing fetus or indirect "sleeper effects" that may only become apparent later (Fried, 1985). Recently, women have reported using marijuana and cocaine to shorten labor (*The Dallas Morning News*, 1989). This may result in delayed development or, in the case of cocaine, withdrawal symptoms at birth.

Densen-Gerber and Rohrs (1981) cite a 1972 report in which the New York State Assembly Select Committee on Child Abuse documented the impact of drug abuse on children, citing four ways that children are victimized by substance abuse:

1. The fetus without prenatal care.
2. The premature, low-birthweight newborn in withdrawal.
3. The helpless neonate sent home with an irresponsible, inadequate, hostile parent.
4. The infant and preschooler neglected by parents and social agencies alike.

1970 statistics indicate that 2,000 heroin addicts in Newark and New Jersey produced 4,500 children under age five. Of 40 births in New York City, one baby is addicted; in Harlem one in 19 is born addicted. Newborns of addicted mothers emit a characteristic, abnormally shrill cry at birth compared to children of non-addicted mothers (Blinick, Tovolga and Antopol, 1977). They also exhibit a significant sleep disturbance (Schulman, 1977) and irritability. Studies show that time of onset and severity of withdrawal symptoms can vary with the mother's dosage, length of addiction, and last use. Suggested treatment of these children is to medically titrate with a similar-acting drug (methadone, diazepam, chlorpromazine, phenobarbital) to prevent severe withdrawal symptoms (Kahn, Neumann and Polk, 1977; Nathenson, Golden and Litt, 1976).

Other studies indicate that withdrawal from heroin during delivery can be dangerous (Rementeria and Nunag, 1973) and that addicts should be maintained rather than withdrawn in late pregnancy. At Philadelphia General Hospital in 1970, a prenatal clinic was instituted that provided comprehensive prenatal care, counseling, and methadone maintenance to known heroin addicts throughout their pregnancy with a drop in neonatal toxemia below the normal population (Finnegan, Connaughton, Emich et al., 1977).

The preceding studies indicate that regardless of which drug in what quantities produces what effect, there is enough evidence in animal (Abel, 1985) and human (Zuckerman, 1985) research to include in prevention messages for pregnant women, information on avoiding cigarettes, alcohol, and any unnecessary drugs during pregnancy. Basic pre- and postnatal education for mothers should include the risks of using teratological substances as well as other **behavioral health risks such as unprotected sex and sharing intra-venous needles as a risk for their child contracting AIDS.** Obvious in all of this research is the conclusion that the behavior of the mother-to-be can have serious consequences for the child and that even before birth the child is affected by the mother's social community context and family.

In the community context, an item of interest is the lack of a public health registry recording FAS incidence that would give more accurate data. This is partially due to the lack of agreement among health care professionals regarding alcohol-related birth defects and the parameters of the diagnostic criteria for FAS, FAE, CFAS and ARBD (Landesman-Dwyer, 1982).

Some medical professionals have expressed skepticism about the research on FAS and substance-related defects. This is unfortunate, when a doctor's credibility could be so useful in spelling out the risks to his patients. The underlying cause of this issue—lack of training of health care professionals in substance abuse—is reflected in a 1980 survey. Dr. Alex Pokorny reported a wide variance in required courses in substance abuse within medical schools, with some schools reporting no required courses outside of the mention of addiction and overdose in a pharmacology course and others requiring 126 hours. This absence of uniformity has been addressed by establishment of the Association of Medical Education and Research in Substance Abuse, which has made rapid progress in standardizing education in this area (Pokorny, 1980).

From the perspective of social policy, some important questions need to be answered regarding FAS and CFAS. The first is the ethical and moral question over the right to abort a pregnancy—when does an individual begin to have rights? Regarding FAS and related defects, what are the rights of two individuals who, in fact, share the same body? If a woman knows the risks of FAS and continues to drink during pregnancy, is this child abuse? Is a heroin-addicted mother by definition unfit? Does a child have the right to be born drug-free? Should society pay for alcohol or drug treatment for women who are at high risk for FAS, or for the child's care if the mother is unable to provide it? Is alcoholism or drug addiction a medical disease or a mental problem and should it be covered by insurance? What is the counseling role and the responsibility of the physician in educating about health risks? How we answer these questions will determine whether we as a society pay now or later for the problem of substance-related birth defects.

The social cost of FAS is difficult to determine due to the lack of definitive research and lack of accurate rates of incidence, but one estimate of the annual cost of direct service to FAS-affected individuals is $2.4 billion based on 1980 figures (NIAAA, 1987).

PRESCHOOL CHILDREN OF SUBSTANCE ABUSERS AND PREVENTION STRATEGIES AND PROGRAMS

A population which is the least visible one affected by alcoholism and substance abuse are preschool children of substance abusers from birth to school age (0-5). There are no figures in the literature that separates children ages zero to five who currently live with an alcoholic parent or parents. The estimated number of children under 18 currently living with an alcoholic parent differs from 12 million to 15 million (Edwards and Zander, 1985), to 6.6 million (Johnson and Bennett, 1988; Bean-Bayog, 1987) with one alcoholic parent, but there are no data that separate children in this age group and few programs that address their needs.

This is possibly the most critical age at which to apply prevention strategies that could aid the family in building the self-esteem, trust, autonomy, and initiative necessary to protect the child from further problems (Naiditch, 1988). It is also with children of this age that the alcoholic parent is most likely to abuse or neglect, and with the most far-reaching consequences. Alcoholism was present in 13 percent of child abuse cases reported in Wisconsin (Kadushin and Martin, 1981). Also, Baumrind (1985) concludes from etiological research that the developmental trajectories of experimental, recreational, and habitual users of illicit drugs may have diverged in the early elementary school years, which means prevention must intervene prior to elementary school. Etiological studies are now beginning to note early childhood attitudes and behavior that may determine, in a broad way, certain health-compromising behaviors in the future. Botvin and Wills (1985) state that the most important information to come from the last ten years of research is that health-compromising behavior seems to be related to underlying causes. The researchers postulate that health promotion programs and the development of personal and social competence could inoculate children against drug use.

The formation of health-related behavior comes through a complex set of influences that begin with the family but may include health care providers, extended family, and television. The interrelated beliefs that a person holds about his/her vulnerability to health problems is also indicative of his/her belief about experiencing other problems. Several persistent correlations are indicated in a cross-section of literature on substance abuse, delinquency, depression, and suicide. These include a sense of powerlessness, low self-esteem, poor interpersonal and social skills, poor academic or vocational performance, negative peer pressure, and poor family relations (Mullen, 1983). Swett (1984) recommends a planned sequential approach beginning in kindergarten and continuing through high school that teaches decision-making skills. This seems to be a reasonable approach, but assumes that young children function cognitively like adults.

In both prevention (Bell & Battjes, 1985) and etiological (Bush and Iannotti, 1985) research there is a caveat regarding grouping children of distinctly different developmental phases into one study. It suggests instead using a cognitive development framework such as Piaget's preoperational (three to six years old), concrete operational (seven to 11 years old), and formal operational (12 and older) as a fundamental consideration in designing materials and programs. The effectiveness and validity of an intervention could be seriously challenged if this is not done. The way a preschool child processes information changes dramatically and quickly. Bush and Iannotti (1985) cite clinical examples of children in the concrete operational stage responding to prevention messages with unique but unintended conclusions.

The Head Start program could be utilized as a channel to promote health concepts and social competence in both minority and low-income families. Head Start is already in place and has a commitment to community initiative, parent involvement, and parent employability (Washington and Oyemade, 1985), and it is specifically targeted to the needs and values of this group. Developing a curriculum and even family support groups on substance abuse and pregnancy risks within Head Start would have economic and cultural advantages over a new program. The fact that there is no specific mention of substance abuse prevention in Head Start literature, however, indicates that some systems need to be linked according to the Systems Linkage Model (Ellis, 1980).

Zigler and Trickett (1978) have advocated social competence rather than IQ change as a more accurate measure of success in Head Start programs and suggests a third order concept of adaptation to subsume both categories. This falls in line with generic social skills training and peer resistance strategies recommended for school-age children of alcoholics to lower their risk factors (Botvin and Wills, 1985). A cost-effective approach to pretesting this hypothesis would be to interview former Head Start participants about their drug and alcohol use, if any (Hawkins, Lishner and Catalano, 1985), and their age of onset, choice of drug, frequency, and amount compared to matched controls, since these groups have been followed statistically for years. It is possible that Head Start has already been practicing the primary prevention of drug and alcohol use but is unaware of it.

Substance abuse prevention programs targeted at preschool children are scarce in the literature, have not existed long, and, thus, have very limited evaluation strategies. None was found that presented statistical data regarding outcome measure, but the programs all deserve some mention due to their theoretical perspective and their useful clinical observations.

Rainbow Days Inc. in Dallas, a nonprofit corporation funded by the Texas Commission on Alcohol and Drug Abuse and private foundations, offers services to children (ages four and older), adolescents, parents, and adult children of alcoholics. "Kid's Connection" groups are separated into preadolescents and adolescents, and parents attend a concurrent but separate group. The group is on an eight-week cycle and has a sliding-scale fee beginning at $75 per cycle for one family member. Rainbow Days also provides group education through an in-school contract for a local school district in cycles of ten sessions.

Sessions center around learning to identify feelings and how to express them appropriately, esteem-building, education about family systems and chemical dependency as a family disease, decision making, and consequences of behavior. The final session is for evaluation of progress, but what kind of evaluation is not specified. The groups try to communicate several messages to clients:

1. You are not alone;
2. Chemical dependency is a disease that affects the whole family;
3. You did not cause, and cannot cure, this dependency;
4. There is hope, families do recover;
5. You are special and deserve help.

This program is primary prevention targeted at the community level by educating preadolescent children about substance abuse. It uses the social inoculation and skill-building approach in the areas of affective education, family systems, and decision making to provide secondary prevention for children at high risk and tertiary prevention for the family system and the parental dyad, as well as adult children who are experiencing problems (from a personal conversation with Jeff Wright at Rainbow Days Inc. on June 30, 1989). The only missing ingredient is an objective evaluation plan to monitor this well-thought-out program.

Another program, Children Are People, formed in 1977, offers workshops for people who want to form support groups for children ages five to 12, awareness groups for the community, and prevention programs to add to school curricula. These children are identified by teachers, church day-care workers, and others who have contact with the child. Techniques include nonverbal game and play therapy as well as teaching coping and safe risk-taking skills. Improving the child's self-esteem and sense of "specialness" are emphasized. School programs are designed to be presented in 30-minute modules by the regular teacher who has had the training (*Alcohol, Drug Abuse, and Mental News*, 1984).

One essential ingredient in any prevention effort directed at children is the inclusion of the parents in the process. Others include the same kind of informational and skill-building approach with emphasis on family interaction training as well as community-based support groups (Swett, 1984).

Chapter III

Prevention Strategies and Programs

PARENTAL PARTICIPATION IN PREVENTION

The one factor that seems to differentiate the children of alcoholic (Blum et al. 1972) and heroin-addicted (Wilson et al., 1980) mothers from similar SES comparison groups is the amount and quality of interaction between the child and the mother. Other factors such as educational level or occupation of parents, age, sex, ethnic group, SES, or participation in school readiness programs were not significant in these studies.

In identifying high-, medium-, and low-risk families for substance abuse, Blum et al. (1972) noted that low-SES black families were intact, Protestant, Democrat, had employed fathers, showed a diversity of interest, shared power, were liberal in some value areas, and trusting of children to make good decisions. Mexican-American low-risk families in the study were poor and shared similar cultural values with high-risk families. The primary difference was in parental attitudes and skill at interaction. Mothers were insightful, confident, flexible, and affectionate. Fathers were active, communicative, and authoritative. Quality of parent/child relationship appears to be one definite independent variable in determining whether a child will use drugs. This has also become an object of research in other fields of mental health, i.e., schizophrenia, and suggests that study of family interaction through an ecological framework may yield a promising path of prevention.

Baumrind (1985) determined three types of parenting styles in a longitudinal study of preschool children and their parents called The Family Socialization and Developmental Competence Project:

1. Authoritarian—high measures of firm enforcement and maturity demands with low measures of warmth and differentiation.
2. Authoritative—high measures of firm enforcement and maturity demands with high measures of warmth and differentiation.
3. Permissive—low on enforcement measures and maturity demands but high on warmth and differentiation.

The children of parents with an authoritative style were consistently and significantly more competent than other children. This suggests that there is a superior style of parenting that impacts a child's competence and can be broken into specific skill sets, and taught. A strategy for prevention with young children is to intervene with the parents and teach them parenting skills based on social learning theory or behavior modification. These interventions are specific, behavior modification techniques that are measurable and designed to maximize parental authority and build in more positive responses to the child for desired behavior.

An example of a program that fits the model of family-centered parent training and also addresses the social context of the family is the ecobehavioral approach to the treatment and prevention of child-abuse and neglect offered through the Illinois Department of Child and Family Services (DCFS) in rural counties of southern Illinois. This program offers up to 15 kinds of services to families that have been charged with child abuse or neglect or are considered high risk.

The program, designed by John R. Lutzker (1984) at Southern Illinois University at Carbondale, fits the Systems Linkage Model by combining Title XX funding and delivery of a broad variety of services with an educational exploration of a treatment model while providing funding and training for students of the Behavior Analysis and Therapy Program.

Services offered include parent/child training, basic skills teaching, health maintenance and nutrition, home safety, marital counseling, stress reduction, money management, leisure time counseling, job-finding, self-control training, alcoholism treatment referral, and an unwed mother program. The approach of addressing as many variables as possible and delivering the services *in situ* fits the Family Intervention Model. Due to the behavioral orientation and high degree of training of the students delivering the services, data collection was accomplished accurately.

The disappointing feature of this program was the reluctance to confront the substance abuse (alcohol) issue as it related to the parents. Clients were referred for community-based treatment but beer was considered an integral part of the culture and had to be "worked around." This program addresses many of the same needs that would be addressed in a substance abuse treatment program that was family-centered; it could with minimum staff training implement a substance abuse component through the current structure. The personal characteristics shared by substance-abusing parents and abusive, neglectful parents are low self-esteem, poor coping skills, feeling socially insular or isolated, marital conflict, and having been abused as a child (Black et al., 1986; Burgess and Richardson, 1984).

Three studies of child abuse and neglect interventions—The Arkansas Project, The Parent and Child Treatment Program, and the University of Michigan Project—all reported successful results using a structural family systems approach but with an emphasis on substance abuse by the parents as a primary problem (*Alcohol, Drug Abuse, and Mental Health News*, 1984). Intervention on the parents as a method to prevent child abuse shows much promise for application to the substance-abusing family. If programs were to include an analysis of drinking behavior and parent characteristics as part of their longitudinal studies, some important information could be revealed regarding the suspected relationship between substance abuse and child abuse and neglect. In fact, parental alcoholism or substance abuse can be considered child abuse. In New York State an adjudicated heroin addict mother is by definition considered unfit (Black, Mayer and MacDonall, 1981). Substance abuse is present in 20 percent to 50 percent of perpetrators of incest (Scavnicky-Mylant, 1984), and significant differences were reported in domestic violence by alcoholic parents and the respondent adult child compared to adult children of nonalcoholic parents (Black, Bucky and Wilder-Padilla, 1986).

A study by McKenna and Pickens (1981) compared the parents of a large sample of chronic alcoholics to determine significant differences between those with one, two, or no alcoholic parents. Results indicated that those with two alcoholic parents were more likely to have been intoxicated at an earlier age, entered treatment at an earlier age, reported more alcohol-related arrests, and exhibited more aggressive behavior than those with one or no alcoholic parents. Those with only an alcoholic father reported more aggressive behavior than those with an alcoholic mother. This study only used subjects who had been raised by both biological parents to control intervening variables, i.e., early loss of a parent, divorce, etc. These studies suggest a relationship between child abuse, parental alcoholism, and general aggressive behavior by all family members. The results of these studies underline the importance of early intervention.

Onset of drug use usually occurs during adolescence when separation anxieties occur in both parents and child. The child attempts to establish an independent identity while the parents promote continued dependence. Drug use allows the child to believe the illusion that he is independent with his drug-using friends while also subverting long-term goals to separate from his parents. Stanton (1980) uses the term "pseudoindividuation" to describe this phenomenon. The family can retain the dysfunctional homeostasis that existed prior to the drug use. The drug user becomes the symptom carrier or identified patient.

Densen-Gerber and Rohrs (1981) recommend that addict parents who refuse intervention receive mandatory treatment until their children are born drug free and must either relinquish their right to them or demonstrate the ability to care for them. This drastic idea is countered by other studies (Black, Mayer et al., 1981) that show methadone-maintained addicts can participate in parent training and show an interest in their children's welfare.

The most intensive area of study has been the impact of alcoholism on children and the potential for problems later in life. There is a paucity of research that studies the impact of other kinds of substance abuse on families or children. Most of this research has been concerned with the effect of the drug (primarily opiates) on the user, and the drug abuser as the child, not the parent. It has also been guided by the erroneous assumption that drug addicts were so consumed by their addiction that they had no families (Stanton et al., 1979). Research in this area revealed that 72 percent of male addicts lived with their mother at age 22 (Stanton, 1980). Much of the literature on drug-abusing family dynamics focuses on the explicit intergenerational coalition between the addict and the opposite-sex parent. The addict remains dependent on his parents but adopts a hostile, aloof manner toward them. Some recurrent distinctive themes in families of heroin addicts are a preponderance of death themes in conversation and the significance of the immigrant status of addicts. The first suggests an incomplete grieving process or suicidal ideations, and the second suggests an incomplete acculturation or acculturation to the drug subculture (Coleman and Stanton, 1981; Coleman, 1981).

Studies on families experiencing alcoholism focus on one or both parents as the substance abuser are characterized by an inconsistent environment and unpredictable reactions by the parents to the children (Hecht, 1973). There are many names for the role relationships in an alcoholic family but clinicians agree on the recurrent pattern of roles played by different family members that helps to maintain a homeostatic family system even at the expense of the growth of the individuals in it (Satir, 1967). The alcoholic's drinking serves as a focus to prevent the family from facing other difficulties such as marital discord, financial problems, or serious emotional problems that may surface in recovery (Straussner, Weinstein, and Hernandez, 1979). Wegscheider (1980) uses the illustration of a hanging mobile to explain the intricate balance of an alcoholic family and how all elements will shift to offset tension caused by the drinking member.

Some concern is expressed in the literature that research on substance-abusing families has been slow to develop due to the fact that insufficient funding often goes to biogenetic and pharmacological studies (Blum, 1980). The complexity of design required in family studies and the reluctance of marriage and family therapists to become involved with substance-abusing families partly due to their own prejudices and the individual focus of much of the research has slowed progress in family research (French, 1987). In research reviewed by Stanton (1980) where family therapy was compared to other modes of treatment, it emerged as superior in two-thirds and equal in the others. The structural approach showed the most impressive results.

Until entering school, a child has little opportunity to be affected by any socialization except that provided by the family. If parents are alcoholic or abuse drugs, the child will be even more socially and emotionally isolated. An erroneous assumption made in some Health Belief Model interventions is that children have the power of autonomous choice in seeking medical attention, selecting food, or that they can make other choices usually made by adults (Bush and Iannotti, 1985). It is this isolation and lack of mobility and autonomy that makes preschool children invisible in the statistics, difficult to identify, and especially vulnerable.

The only alternative socialization for many preschool children of substance abusers is television. Hazelden (1989) estimates that a child sees 1 million television ads between birth and drinking age and 10 percent of those are for beer. Children between two and five watch approximately 33.5 hours of television a week. In one year, children see 20,000 commercials. Although "Sesame Street" and other programs have a positive impact, there is concern that television's influence on children's choice of food, use of over-the-counter drugs, and aggressive behavior may be negative (Mullen, 1983). Mullen suggests:

1. Limiting certain promotional techniques.
2. A ban on certain types of advertising and behavior.
3. Limiting the number of commercials for given types of products.
4. Health warnings within a commercial.
5. Provision for free counter-advertising under a fairness doctrine.
6. Periodic monitoring by governmental agencies of television content for use in informing the public.
7. Teaching critical viewing skills to children.

Prevention programs in the media have not proven very effective in changing health behaviors. This spells out the continued need for evaluation of public service messages to avoid expensive mistakes (Mullen, 1983). Research indicates the importance of evaluating a target audience's knowledge, attitudes, and behaviors in order to plan effective communication (Bandy and President, 1983).

Alternatives to television for preschool and child-care personnel and parents are the many emerging children's activity/coloring books that describe alcoholic families. The cognitive abilities of the children should be considered in selecting these books. The denial and shame experienced by children of alcoholics may be broken down by identification with an intermediary character in a book. The psychotherapeutic stages of identification, projection, catharsis, and insight may help the child's self-identify and may also help form new opinions about his or her parents' behavior. Books mentioned (Manning, 1987) for younger children include *My Dad Loves Me, My Dad Has a Disease* (1979), Claudia Black; *Pepper* (1974), Elaine Melquist; *Sometimes My Mom Drinks Too Much* (1980), Kevin Kenny and Helen Krull, and others. No books were mentioned for children of drug-addicted parents, nor were evaluation procedures offered to judge the effectiveness of this approach.

SOME IDENTIFYING FACTORS OF CHILDREN IN NEED

When a child enters school, subtle behavior patterns can be recognized to identify him as from an alcoholic or substance-abusing home. These could be formalized into an instrument to aid teachers and counselors in identifying children needing help. It should be kept in mind here that teachers should be trained in the use of the instrument, and not be allowed to arbitrarily determine that certain children are from substance-abusing homes. These behaviors mirror the inconsistent homelife (Edwards and Zander, 1985):

1. Fluctuations in the child's personal appearance or health.
2. Wide variations in academic or task performance for no apparent reason.
3. Exaggerated concern with pleasing teachers or authority figures.
4. Tardiness or poor attendance.
5. Fear of parent/teacher conferences.

6. Social isolation from peers.
7. Negative attitude displayed toward drinking in drug education classes as well as mature knowledge of types of alcohol and drinks.

Recognition of preschool children in need should be accomplished through social agencies that have contact with parents seeking treatment for alcoholism and addiction, through the family courts, the police, child protection services, and preschool programs like Head Start. Care should be taken not to further stigmatize the family or children or discriminate against minorities in identifying and treating this population.

In special need of assistance are low-income children of substance-abusing families. Drug use is more prevalent among dropouts than among those in school (National Institute on Drug Abuse, 1987). Minorities and the disadvantaged have a higher dropout rate (Hahn, Danzberger, and Lefkowitz, 1987). This corresponds roughly to the adult illiteracy rate, 44 percent of all Afro-Americans, 56 percent of all Hispanic Americans, and 16 percent of all Caucasians (Editorial Research Reports, 1985). Minorities are more likely to be poor. "Median white net wealth, $39,135 in 1984, was almost twelve times greater than that of black households, $3,397 . . . ," states Bell (1987), while "three tenths of black households had no assets at all or were in debt as compared with only one twelfth of white households." Afro-Americans, Hispanic Americans, and Native Americans all are more likely than Caucasians to be poor, to have less education, and to be in poorer health.

Children "are far more likely these days to be poor than any other age group. . . . Almost half of all black children are poor, as are over a third of Hispanic children. But despite their lower rate, 16.9 in 1983, the 8.5 million poor white children dominate the group" (Bell, 1987). The Children's Defense Fund, which has done stellar work, states (1988):

• Children make up the poorest age group in America. One in four of all preschoolers and one in five of all children are poor; among children born into single-parent households, one in two is poor; among the children of teenage single mothers, 84.4

percent are poor; and among children with two parents younger than 22, one in three is poor. More than 43 percent of all black children and 37.7 percent of all Hispanic children are poor.

- American children, America's future, are 1.7 times more likely to be poor than adults older than 65, 2.1 times more likely to be poor than adults older than 55, and 2.5 times more likely to be poor than adults older than 45.

It is known that substance abuse occurs among all ethnic groups and social classes. But we aver that substance abuse occurs disproportionately among minorities and low income populations. Native Americans, for example, "have rates of alcohol abuse and alcoholism several times higher than rates in the general population" (National Institute on Alcohol Abuse and Alcoholism, 1987). Drug abuse is now more of a problem among lower income groups (as is AIDS). Compounding these problems are the ineffective services available to minority and low-income substance abusers. While substance abuse services (particularly for alcoholism) proliferate for the middle and upper classes, substance abuse services for the poor are often spotty, ill-funded, and inadequate. As Richard Titmuss has said, services to the poor are almost inevitably poor services.

Numerous socioeconomic factors determine whether substance-abusing mothers and their offspring will be able to receive treatment, the largest factor being the current American health insurance crisis. Poor substance-abusing parents of preschool children are more likely to be uninsured and, hence, unable to afford expensive substance abuse treatment. Treatment of this population may be even more expensive because of the need for child care and for other support services, economic and otherwise.

We would argue for major antipoverty programs that would increase economic opportunities of the poor relative to that of the affluent (Titmuss, 1968). We think that substance abuse among low-income populations, and health problems in general, would be reduced by such actions. Especially helped would be the tremendous number of minority or low-income substance abusers.

SCHOOL-BASED PREVENTION PROGRAMS

The broadest range of programs for preventing drug abuse is offered through schools beginning in elementary school and continuing through high school. Since onset of drug use usually occurs in this developmental stage, much attention has gone to prevention in this period. According to Hawkins, Lishner and Catalano, 1985, school-based programs have been aimed at preventing:

1. "Abuse" defined as pathological use;
2. Regular use of legal but health-compromising substances (tobacco);
3. Any use of psychoactive substances;
4. First use at an early age.

In programs that attempt to segment children of substance-abusing families from other kids, the emphasis needs to be on abstinence and delaying onset. In family education programs the correlated risk factors of intergenerational chemical dependency should be stressed to children of substance abusers.

The variety, frequency, and intensity of antisocial behaviors occurring in early childhood can predict an array of problems in adolescence that can continue into adulthood. Drug use, marijuana use, drinking, and some other behaviors can all be predicted from early antisocial behavior sometimes called "deviance syndrome." Inconsistent and unorganized families with poorly defined rules are a major variable in predicting child behavior problems (Hawkins et al., 1985). On the other hand, strong positive family relationships and attachment seem to discourage drug use. These findings point to programs that strengthen the family as the optimum focus of prevention efforts. Unfortunately, government funding for family programs has been sorely inadequate. This leaves the burden of carrying the prevention messages to the school system.

The advantage of school-based prevention programs is the long-term continuous contact they have with children and a nearly complete coverage of children from five to 18. Early in American education, health promotion was considered a basic subject; the formally structured, supportive atmosphere offers children from substance-abusing families an alternative model. Also, the children are evaluated through testing and observation over long periods and problems can be identified.

An intervention designed for five- to 12-year-olds is the Sunshine Clubs offered in grades one through six through the Tarrant Council on Alcoholism and Drug Abuse, Fort Worth. These eight-week support groups are delivered in 45-minute sessions either during or after school and feature such topics as self-esteem, feelings, friendships, problem-solving, decision making, and coping with chemical abuse in the family. Students are referred by teachers, counselors, or themselves but must have parental approval to attend (Student club . . . , 1989). Parental approval can become a difficult issue with programs that identify as being for children of substance-abusing parents instead of being a generic health promotion program.

An effective program that combines a community-based drug and alcohol agency with the school system is the Alpha Model of treatment, which serves high-risk elementary school populations. Participants may not be currently abusing substances but exhibit high-risk behaviors such as low achievement, insufficient self-control and motivation, disruptive behavior, and feelings of alienation. The student is taught in a special environment away from regular classes, one that is managed by a contingency method of granting privileges based on earned points for desired behavior. This program also has parent training and training and reinforcements for the teachers. Children remain in classes two days a week. After two years of evaluation, participants showed significant improvement in academics, attention, impulse control, aggressiveness, and social conformity on the Burks Behavior Rating Scale (Landress, 1983).

As children develop past sixth grade, several issues become salient in preventing drug abuse:

1. They begin to be influenced more by their peers than by authority;
2. They experiment with risk-taking behavior;
3. They begin to be exposed to drug and alcohol use by other adolescents or siblings.

As mentioned, drug use statistically is no longer aberrant for this age group, and distinctions need to be made in defining use, abuse, and addiction. The family and the adolescent experience anxiety as the adolescent becomes more independent and begins the maturing process of leaving home. Most adolescents experiment with alcohol or cigarettes first and hard drugs later. Some adolescents use only a few times and quit. Others may use more regularly but "mature out" as they reach adulthood. The research in this area has focused on antecedent personality traits, skills, type of drug first used, and age of onset.

The most important predictors of onset of drug use parallel characteristics associated with children from substance abusing families. These include early age of onset, deviant behavior, low self-esteem, and poor academic performance. One variable that appears to have mixed results is the social skill level of the adolescent. Since first drug use occurs in social situations, a socially mature adolescent may be pressured into use by older children who would not be part of the peer group of a less mature child. On the other hand, alienation and poor social and assertiveness skills are often significant predictors of pathological drug use in adolescents (Baumrind, 1985).

The school-based programs that address these issues are too numerous to mention but share many of the same underlying theoretical frameworks. The work of Evans based on Bandura's social learning theory and Macguire's communication theory—described by Botvin and Wills (1985) as "psychological inoculation"— teaches children specific strategies to resist peer pressure to use drugs. This is accompanied by broader based assertiveness or social competence training that includes decision-making, coping skills, and affective education to reduce the impact of anxiety and lack of self-efficacy that may create a desire in the child to use drugs.

Segal (1986) describes three motives for drug-taking gleaned from an in-depth study of 1,500 students from grades 7 to 12 in Alaska:

1. A "coping" motive;
2. A "drug experience" motive;
3. A "peer-influence" motive.

These motives indicate expressed needs of adolescents that could be met by means other than taking drugs. The first need for coping skills is not only an adolescent need but is an area of concern for parents, adults, and mental health care professionals and appears to be a significant focus of prevention in any stress-related illness. The second motive expresses a strong adolescent need to encounter risks in order to test identity and self-efficacy. To thwart this natural developmental phenomenon through rigid and overprotective rules and standards may result in more rebellious behavior. The third motive of peer pressure becomes more difficult because adolescents begin to seek guidance from each other rather than adults. Also, once a child begins to use drugs he begins to rely on drug-using peers for information and values about drugs (Baumrind, 1985). Effective prevention programs should seriously consider the development of peer leaders for groups of adolescents. Obviously a school-based program for adolescents should consider and address these specific problems as well as the primary prevention messages already mentioned for younger children.

The CASPAR program was developed as an outgrowth of the Cambridge-Somerville Mental Health and Retardation Program when it received an NIAAA grant in 1974. A community-based program, it begins with 20-hour workshops for elementary and secondary school teachers, counselors, and administrators featuring interactive group techniques to challenge and identify attitudes, biases, and myths held by participants about alcohol use. The school-based component is a series of one-hour expandable teaching modules sequentially and developmentally geared to children from grades K-12. Key features contribute to the effectiveness of the program:

1. Teacher training in alcohol education and group skills.
2. Group work focusing on interactive discussion of peers rather than a didactic lecture.
3. Training and use of students as group leaders and evaluation assistants.
4. Community component raising community awareness of alcohol issues.

The success of this program has resulted in many replications. In 1982 the Department of Education made it the first alcohol education program chosen for the DOE's National Diffusion Network (NIAAA, 1983).

A school-based program that combines drug and alcohol education selected by NIAAA is the "Here's Looking at You, Two." It was selected due to its comprehensive, long-term sequential teaching modules and the teacher training it provides. It also was thoroughly field tested with good results. This program emphasizes teaching self-awareness skills, including effective skills in recognizing and expressing feelings. It also emphasizes coping and problem-solving skills (NIAAA, 1983).

Few studies of education programs "have even attempted to show influences on drinking/drug use behaviors and even fewer have observed significant effects on these behaviors (again, some of these have found negative effects)" (Braucht and Braucht, 1984). The researchers add that "severe and pervasive methodological flaws in the extant evaluation studies make *any* conclusions regarding the effectiveness of alcohol/drug-use educational strategies more a matter of reliance on faith than on credible empirical evidence." One area that needs to be researched would be the effectiveness of preschool substance abuse education programs.

Current research does not lend as much credence to the effectiveness of substance abuse education programs as the proponents of such strategies might like. Even more thorough, comprehensive evaluations of substance abuse education programs are needed. Researchers should try different techniques with different populations and evaluate the results. It would appear that early prevention programs should focus on health promotion and wellness rather than health risks and illness. But, again, this needs to be researched thoroughly. Indeed, unique populations may require unique approaches: A substance abuse education program in an Afro-American community in the rural Mississippi delta region may look quite different from a substance abuse education program in an Afro-American community in urban Newark, NJ. Globetti (1989) says it would appear that "strategies derived from both the developmental and sociocultural models would be particularly relevant to the minority community. . . . Programs for these populations should be more in tune with the whole 'life situation' than with just problem drinking, which is usually a symptom of personal and cultural disjunctions exacerbated by minority status."

Future research should be guided by the question, "What kinds of educational strategies have what kinds of effects on what kinds of young people?" (Braucht and Braucht, 1984). Some factors would be: age differences (age four, in a child-care program, vs. a 17-year-old secondary school student), gender differences, ethnicity differences, social class differences, residence (urban vs. rural) differences, religious differences, previous experiences with substance use or abuse (children of alcoholics vs. children of teetotalers), and personality differences. Most important would be the mix of the above and the effectiveness of substance abuse education. By mix we mean, for example, a five-year-old, urban, middle-class Cuban boy and, say, a five-year-old, rural, low-income Mexican-American girl — what might an effective substance abuse education program look like in respect to both children? We could throw in family experience with substance abuse, religious background, and other variables, and we can see how complicated this area is.

Research needs to focus on how systems can come together to establish a single agency that can deliver an array of services. Child abuse, sexual abuse, substance abuse, domestic violence, divorce, and criminal behavior are often present in the same families but require intervention from several agencies. This reductionistic approach is ineffective and inefficient.

Enough evidence exists to make the dissemination of community and school-based substance abuse prevention programs a major national priority. The basic framework of the STARR Project or the Under One Roof program would possibly translate to other communities.

No research instrument may be sophisticated enough to provide all the information needed. But we must have some kind of information (however crude), which makes it seminal to obtain more and better research on the effectiveness of preschool and school-based substance abuse education programs.

COMMUNITY-BASED PREVENTION PROGRAMS FOR ADOLESCENTS

Both of these programs and most other effective programs include a community- and family-based component. As expressed by the three models outlined at the beginning of this work, drug abuse prevention must operate on the community and family level in order to be effective. Prevention programs such as the "Under One Roof" program in Chisago County, MN, is an example of a program that involves the entire community. This ambitious program has attempted to change community norms regarding substance abuse and has been able to measure changes in attitudes, age at first use, and frequency of drinking in adolescents (Hazelden, 1989). The program was not directed from an agency or health care institution but was disseminated through schools, churches, law enforcement agencies, and parents. The fundamental goal of the program is to communicate to all the children in the community three messages:

1. You do not have to use chemicals to be who you want to be.
2. You can say no to chemicals and still have fun and friends.
3. There are people in the community who care about you and what you will become.

The primary work of the program was to train a core group in different institutions in the community about the messages to be conveyed, but how those messages were delivered was left up to each group. Community-based programs and social support for parents and kids are empowering components that promote community health goals and prevent the target population from being stigmatized as "the problem."

The new public health view of drug problems has been the result of an increasing awareness of self-inflicted, health-compromising behaviors and a re-evaluation of social values concerning the availability of alcohol, tobacco, and over-the-counter drugs. This heightened awareness is a result of the dissemination of information and has resulted in legislation that limits smoking behavior and requires tobacco labeling. The current area of contention is the labeling and availability of alcohol. The liquor industry is firmly resisting the acceptance of this public health position and the requirement of warning labels either on the product or at the point of sale (Blume, 1987). There is a return to viewing the control of availability of alcohol as one form of prevention. Beauchamp (1976) discusses, as myth, the belief that alcoholics are defective in some way and that others can drink safely and compares this to heroin addiction as being the fault of the addict. There are bad drugs but with alcohol it is the user who is to "blame." The issue of labeling is being tested in the courts; with cigarettes as a precedent, it seems that labeling is on its way to reality. Whether anyone actually changes their behavior due to a warning label remains to be seen.

The Sumner Tobacco and Alcohol Risk Reduction (STARR) Project combined the "Here's Looking at You, Two" with a peer helping program and a parent training program as well as a community-based component that included these five strategies:

1. Offer "natural highs," alternative activities to alcohol and drug use.
2. Provide positive role models.
3. Provide vendor education.
4. Use the mass media.
5. Provide opportunities to involve law enforcement in prevention programs.

The organization and involvement of members of a community around an issue can act as an empowering and supportive force regardless of the issue. This is particularly true in a low-income or minority area where the pervasive feelings of powerlessness can undermine prevention efforts of individual families or school programs. The Oakland Parents in Action group is an example of community organizing efforts that paid off with safer neighborhoods, a firm school policy regarding drug use, parent and community networks, and an improved relationship with law enforcement (NIDA, 1986). These programs are well-documented and serve as models for many other programs aimed at early intervention or prevention.

FAMILY INTERVENTION AND TREATMENT

In addressing the needs of substance abusing families, several questions emerge that should be considered in designing programs. What is the unit of intervention: The substance abuser? The enabling spouse or parent? The children? The family system? To use the metaphor popularized by Wegscheider (1980), the substance-abusing family, like a mobile, is interconnected and intervention on one will result in adaptation by the other family members. This suggests that intervention can occur at any level, with any member, provided that the intervention is potent enough to offset the negative impact of the family system on the substance abuser and that the interactions within the family change enough to promote growth.

One recent implementation that has altered treatment for substance abuse is the involvement of family members in the treatment process of recovering substance abusers. The involvement of the spouse in the alcoholic's recovery from alcoholism and the inherent problems encountered by both are detailed in the book *Alcoholics Anonymous* (1939).

> Cessation of drinking is but the first step away from a highly strained, abnormal condition. A doctor said to us, "Years of living with an alcoholic is almost sure to make any wife or child neurotic. The entire family is to some extent ill." The alcoholic may find it hard to re-establish friendly relations with his children. Their young minds were impressionable while he was drinking. Without saying so, they may cordially hate him for what he has done to them and their mother. The children are sometimes dominated by a pathetic hardness and cynicism. They cannot seem to forgive and forget.

These comments were made from observing the early families recovering through Alcoholics Anonymous and resulted in the formation of Al-Anon and later Alateen as separate organizations addressing the specific needs of those who have lived with an alcoholic. The current explosion of literature on the subject has resulted in many of the current top best-selling books addressing an aspect of codependency or co-alcoholism.

A study by Edwards (1982) revealed a relationship between a spouse's participation in a family program and the alcoholic's recovery. The greater number of sessions attended by the spouse, the more likely the alcoholic was to complete treatment and not re-enter treatment. When alcoholics or substance abusers cease practicing their primary addiction they often still suffer from codependency, the same dysfunction as their spouses, with an impaired ability to maintain an intimate relationship. A different explanation by Bepko (1984) suggests that the overcompensation of the spouse to offset the underfunctioning of the alcoholic is difficult to reverse in recovery unless both spouses are involved in treatment. She suggests in a more recent article (1988) that there are gender-specific issues in alcoholism treatment and that women are socialized to show dependence and hide autonomy while men are socialized to show autonomy and hide dependence and that alcoholic drinking allows both partners to suppress or express impulses that run counter to their socialization.

The most often mentioned model for treatment of these families is family systems therapy, with structural family systems theory considered the most effective explanation for the interaction observed in these families. The primary block to delivering this treatment is the denial of the family that they have a problem. The alcoholic has become the identified patient and his or her drinking the identified problem (Henderson, 1985), but the proficient therapist must be able to look beyond the obvious to find the underlying problems (Kaslow, 1980). If there is a problem in the marital relationship then an avoidance of that problem by forming a triangulation either with an abusable substance or an inappropriate intergenerational alliance with another family member will allow the problem to go unresolved and maintain the family homeostasis (Rothberg, 1986).

Several parent training programs focus on preventing substance abuse by strengthening family cohesiveness. One example is the Kumpfer/DeMarsh Family Skills Training Program that combines play therapy with communication skills training. This program demonstrated improvements in the area of family functioning, children's behavior problems, and children's expressiveness (DeMarsh and Kumpfer, 1986). Most family prevention programs build skills in behavioral control, effective expression, or cognitive/communication.

Interventions on the family may be focused at the marital dyad, on the parent child interaction, and parents supporting each other. Parent support groups have been instrumental in mobilizing community resources, providing a supportive network, and empowering their families to resist the threat of substance abuse.

Chapter IV

Children of Minority Groups
and Substance Abuse

There has been relatively little research or literature on substance abuse among minorities in general, and considerably less on substance abuse among minority families with preschool children in the home. Many of these families consist of a single parent. The word "minority" includes such a vast, disparate population, including such diverse populations as reservation Native Americans, urban blacks, and many others, that any research or literature must be prefaced by many qualifications. Brisbane (1985:179) notes that black children experience problems with traditional therapies where talking and self-disclosure are employed. This is a statement that would certainly apply to Native Americans, and probably in various ways to most minority populations. But, there are many nuances here, as there are with any statement about any amorphous group of people. What is important here is sensitizing policies and services (and people) to cultural and minority issues and differences (and nuances). This chapter will address the role of cultural and minority issues and children of substance abusing families.

THE ROLE OF CULTURAL ISSUES
IN SERVICE DELIVERY TO CHILDREN
OF ALCOHOLIC FAMILIES*

The Southern Community Mental Health Center in Texas has a mandate to serve several communities. Its client population in-

---

*This is slightly revised from: National Institute on Alcohol Abuse and Alcoholism, *How to Provide Services for Children from Alcoholic Families*, Rockville, Maryland, 1985, Chapter IV "The Role of Cultural Issues in Service Delivery to Children of Alcoholic Families," pp. 26-35.

cludes a range of ethnic groups. After attending a regional conference on reaching minority clients, the director of the Center decides to hire a minority consultant. The consultant's job will be to develop contacts within these diverse groups, publicize the Center's services, and train Center staff in effective service delivery.

At the first training session, the staff members have an opportunity to describe how well they think the Center is serving its clientele. One alcoholism professional objects to the training. "I don't think we should put so much effort into reaching these people. They come in one time during a family crisis. They expect us to solve all their problems immediately. After investing a good amount of time in intake interviews and scheduling appointments, we never see them again. I think it's a waste of time to be concerned about these clients who won't be responsible for their own health."

The consultant responds, "You have made an important contribution to this session. We know that minority clients interrupt their treatment more frequently than other clients. They have a lower 'rate of return' for treatment, as it were. If they are not showing up for their first clinical session, there must be something happening in that intake interview to discourage them. Let's take a look at what information is exchanged and how it is exchanged during that initial contact with the agency. For example, how did you talk about alcoholism? How did you refer to the family involvement in the treatment plan? Being sensitive to each client's view of alcoholism, self, and family may yield greater success in keeping the client in treatment. That is what we are here to discuss."

FOCUS QUESTIONS

What are the cultural issues affecting service delivery? How does the existing health system meet the needs of a variety of clients? Are unique, culturally based programs required?

INTRODUCTION

Throughout this review, it has been emphasized that children of alcoholics learn certain attitudes and values concerning family, themselves, and alcohol through the interaction in their families.

The purpose of this chapter is to explain how cultural patterns of behavior learned by alcoholic families through interaction in cultural communities affect the different ways they seek and respond to service delivery. The caregiver concerned with the children of alcoholic families needs to understand family and cultural issues before intervening with or treating the child. Strategies of education and treatment depend on such understanding. Therefore, this chapter reviews some of the understanding provided by present and past research in the following areas:

- What function does alcohol serve in the cultural group?
- How does the cultural group regard alcoholism?
- What role do the members of the family and cultural community play in the treatment or prevention of alcoholism?

Each of these areas will be addressed for Native Americans, Hispanic Americans, and black Americans.

Little comparative cultural information on children of alcoholics was found. Therefore, the following discussion is focused broadly on the family and cultural group. Where appropriate, information specifically relevant to the children in emphasized.

WHAT ARE THE CULTURAL ISSUES AFFECTING SERVICE DELIVERY?

Native Americans

What function does alcohol serve? Many theories exist concerning the function of alcohol in the Native American culture. Some theories are based on observations of different tribes by anthropologists and sociologists. Others are based on the experiences of nonnative health providers and law enforcement officials who come into contact with alcohol abusers. What is important to remember is that there are "482 different and separate tribes recognized by the Federal Government" (NIDA, 1977) in the United States whose members are in urban and rural settings (NIAAA, 1980a). Each tribe has a unique history of development of cultural patterns and interaction with Spanish, French, and English settlers and explorers of this country. The evolution of patterns of alcohol use is a part of this history.

A review by Waddell and Everett (1980) of four anthropological studies of southwest Indian tribes highlights the historical variation in alcohol use. Some Native American groups incorporated alcohol use in hunting and agricultural rituals and in social events long before Europeans introduced alcohol as a trading medium in the sixteenth and seventeenth centuries. Other Indian groups claim external forces — for example, the development of settlements and urban bars near reservations — were responsible for the use of alcohol by their members. When some Indian leaders expressed concern that alcohol abuse would become a major problem for their people, Congress prohibited liquor sales to and among the Indians in 1832 (NIAAA, 1980a). This legislation was not repealed until 1953. Even today, there are more reservations where this prohibition remains the rule than reservations where liquor sales are allowed, although bootlegging is a substantial problem on most "dry" reservations (Will Foster, personal communication, March, 1982).

Native Americans face unique life decisions among the minorities living in the United States. Cultural behaviors are integral to life within an Indian tribe. As a result, leaving the tribal community often involves accepting the values and behavior patterns of other cultures. Decisions about where to work and where to establish homes bring many Indian peoples face to face with unemployment and discrimination, whether the choice is between the isolation of living on a reservation or in a white community. The need to cope when the unpredictable way of life, the need to become acculturated to other non-Indian life styles, and the need to experience shared frustration have been identified as factors supporting a pattern of heavy drinking behavior.

Conflict over life decisions leads to the difficulty many Indian peoples experience in maintaining ties with their own tribes or developing new ones with white communities. The development of ties in a community through participation and achievement of socially desirable goals is called developing a "stake." Ferguson (1976) identifies the low degree of "stake" development in Indian and white communities as an explanation of heavy drinking, the recognition of which is a factor in successful alcoholism treatment programs. In an analysis of an alcoholism treatment program for a group of Navajo Indians arrested for drunkenness, Ferguson found that those with steady employment, homeownership, and involvement in both Indian and white communities had the highest treatment success rate.

In many Indian groups, drinking performs the function of binding social groups of peers. Drinking behavior is learned in social situations with one's peer group. Drinking groups often appear to be formed along age lines, that is, older men drink together and young men drink together. According to anthropological studies, these age groups may have different perspectives on the purpose and style of their drinking. The older group is more tranquil; the younger is more aggressive and boisterous, using drinking to support risk-taking behavior (Waddell and Everett, 1980). In some Indian groups (e.g., Navajos and Papagos) there is a great deal of verbal pressure to convince abstainers to join in. One form of verbal pressure is the claim that drinking is identified with what is Indian. Even if people cannot afford to contribute alcohol or money, they are welcomed and encouraged to drink when the occasion arises (Escalante, 1980; Waddell and Everett, 1980).

Indian groups have established norms to distinguish between appropriate and inappropriate heavy drinking patterns. The primary distinction concerns group versus solitary drinking and the effect of each on family members. Drinking with one's peers and during particular events is accepted. Therefore, as long as one's drinking behavior is consistent with the values of the tribe, it is not considered alcohol abuse. However, drinking that is solitary and "selfish," lacking regard for one's peers and one's family obligations, is cause for concern.

How does the cultural group regard alcoholism? Tribal use of alcohol and culturally acceptable drinking behaviors vary. However, the Native American concept of alcoholism differs from the white concept on the issue of origin. Many Indian peoples regard illness as spiritual, not physical, in origin. Alcoholism is considered a disorder of the spirit, as is mental illness. In fact, some older traditional Indians perceive alcoholism to be the same thing as insanity. In this context, even violent behavior during heavy drinking is seldom penalized. The concept of alcoholism is understood to be an white one.

It is difficult for an Indian to face identification as an alcoholic, as this process brings two cultural views into conflict. By identifying oneself as an alcoholic, one seems to be accepting the values of the white culture. At the same time, as a Native American, self-identification as an alcoholic is regarded as admitting a wrongdoing or weakness. The condition of alcoholism is seen as a punishment by supernatural forces. Since self-identification as an alcoholic is an important step in receiving treatment, cultural aspects of alcoholism should be viewed as a crucial factor in planning service delivery approaches.

What role do the family and community play concerning the alcoholic? The role of the family in Native American life and the interaction between Indian families and neighboring communities of non-Indians are critical elements in providing services to Indian alcoholic families. Historically, the extended family has been the cultural group that handles decision making, economic maintenance, and reciprocal obligations (Cooley, 1980). Allegiance is owed to one's own family, and not necessarily to neighboring families or even to the tribe. Roles, values, anticipated occupations, and memberships in social groups are transmitted within one's family. Therefore, the members of one's extended family are crucial to education, development, and support in the case of illness. This cultural answer to handling problems indicates that a direct application of traditional white health care programs to Indian alcoholics may not be successful.

Another factor in effective service delivery to Native Americans is the relationship of Indian groups to neighboring non-Indian communities. As non-Indian bureaucracies and service institutions have developed in urban areas and on some reservations, these institutions have become a source of new drinking behavior standards for Native Americans. Many Indian reservations are near border towns in which it is legal to drink. Many States have decriminalized public intoxication and even provide local alcoholism and reception centers for the intoxicated. In these States, Indians leave the reservation to drink in town, knowing that they will be free of judicial sanctions and will have a safe place to dry out. Unfortunately, most communities that have decriminalized public intoxication consider the drinking problem to be an Indian problem alone. Therefore, there is little financial support for either alcoholism prevention, treatment programs, or cultural centers where Indians may be involved in alternative productive and stimulating social activities (Wood, 1980). In States without decriminalization laws, an intoxicated Indian is often more harshly treated than an equally inebriated white resident.

Due to the lack of support from many white communities, Native Americans must rely on their own resources at the tribe and family level to combat the effects of alcoholism on the alcoholic and the family. The Native American culture traditionally prescribes specialist roles for tribal members, such as healers and educators. These traditional caregivers, together with family members and Native Americans trained as alcoholism specialists, can work with the alcoholic and family to foster an understanding of the disease of alcoholism and develop prevention and treatment programs consistent with Native American philosophies of health.

Culturally based and supported prevention programs are especially important for Native American children of alcoholics (Will Foster, personal communication, March, 1982; Mason, 1982). According to a recent National Council on Alcoholism position paper (1980), 80 percent of Native American college students and 50 percent of high school students drop out due to family alcoholism. This is only one of the effects felt by these children.

Children in alcoholic Native American families hear conflicting messages about the use of alcohol. As a result they are confused over whether to drink and how much to drink. Children see the drinking behavior of male family members accepted. Both aggressive and recreational behaviors are associated with alcohol abuse. Parents do not bother children over the age of 18 who drink (Mason, 1982). Because children of alcoholics are more likely to become alcoholics, the perpetuation of role models of alcohol abuse can only compound the Native American youth's chances of becoming an alcoholic. It is easy to see how alcohol abuse can become the number one health problem among Native Americans.

Alcohol education programs that have a principal goal of countering the cultural attitudes toward alcohol use and abuse may be the most useful response for Native American children of alcoholics (Will Foster, personal communication, March, 1982). Mason (1982) recommends the school as the ideal setting to confront these attitudes. She further advises that education focused broadly on decision making and coping skills would be more acceptable to children and to the school than intervention by an alcoholism specialist.

The teacher who possesses facts about alcohol use and other youth problems can work with parents, bringing them into the classroom or working with them at home, to participate in "saying no" skill development activities with their children. Ideally, these skills would provide the basis for helping youth to resist peer group pressure which might be exerted to use or abuse alcohol.

Hispanic Americans

What function does alcohol serve? There are many different nationalities of Hispanic persons living in the United States or immigrating to find employment and to join families already here. These nationalities include Mexicans, Cubans, Dominicans, Puerto Ricans, and Guatemalans. Although there has been limited research on Hispanic alcoholism and alcohol use, and virtually nothing on children of Hispanic alcoholics, what is available shows that there are differences in Spanish American populations by national origin, racial background, Spanish-speaking ability, socioeconomic level, and degree of acculturation (Sanchez-Dirks, 1978). Any discussion of general Hispanic patterns of alcohol use is therefore limited, corresponding to the limited findings about different groups.

In general (Gordon, 1979; Parachini, 1981; Rodriguez et al., 1979; Sierra, 1981; and Technical Systems Institute, 1980), researchers have found that members of Hispanic populations drink heavily or not at all. When excessive drinking by either men or women prevents individuals from meeting their responsibilities, it is viewed negatively by family and community.

Definitions of acceptable and unacceptable alcohol-related behavior may vary among groups and across locales and situations. Myths regarding cultural patterns of alcohol use are one of the targets of researchers and clinicians now working with the Hispanic alcoholic family. The goal is to identify actual patterns of alcohol use and incorporate them in elements of program development and the training of caregivers working with the family and with children.

How does the cultural group regard alcoholism? It is widely believed that the male Hispanic is regarded as head of his family and that this role is carried over to social situations. That is, the male is regarded as the authority within the family and the community. The term "machismo" refers to the male's ability to support his family and maintain its economic independence. Success in the economic sphere entitles the male to drink with friends freely. Peer groups drink together after work and during social events. If the male Hispanic has problems related to his drinking behavior, his family tends to blame the problems on fate, God's will, or a bad wife (Romero, n.d.). The tendency to avoid the health issues of alcoholism may vary, however, according to the degree of acceptance of white values by the Hispanic and his family.

The concept of male dominance in the Hispanic culture is being disputed (Andrade, 1980). It may be that decision making in the home is really dominated by the female Hispanic. However, the concern for the image of the male within his extended family and community leads to a general portrayal of the male as head of the household. This extends to an avoidance by the female and children of seeking help outside the community for problems. There is an effort to protect the image of the male even when his alcoholism may be affecting the economic life of the family.

Hispanic women are expected to fulfill the important roles of wife and mother. After they have raised their families, women attain a certain status as "mother," which allows them to be involved in their children's families. According to Romero (n.d.) the process of attaining this status involves giving up a woman's individuality for the sake of the family. This creates serious problems for the female Hispanic alcoholic.

The Hispanic woman is not supposed to embarrass her "people," which includes her husband's mother and family as well as her own. If a woman has alcohol-related problems, she receives less family support for treatment and rehabilitation than a man would (Romero, n.d.; Technical Systems Institute, 1980). Her problems are blamed on her lack of dedication to traditional roles. Unlike the male alcoholic, no one makes excuses for her. People advise the Hispanic woman not to stay away from her family and therefore do not encourage involvement in treatment programs that separate her from the family. As a result, although traditional Hispanic women may drink less than those who have accepted the values of the white culture, those who have alcohol-related problems come into treatment later and remain for a shorter period of time.

From an analysis of a survey on drinking practices of youth, Sanchez-Dirks (1978) reports certain characteristics or patterns of drinking among Hispanic youth. No information was available for analysis on the use of alcohol by Hispanic children of alcoholics.

Hispanic youth living with both parents drink less than youth living with their fathers only. However, when asked about the effect of their parents' attitudes toward drinking on their own drinking habits, Hispanic youth said they value their friends' opinions more than their parents'. These youth also showed themselves to be higher consumers of alcohol than the youth who value their parents' opinions.

For Hispanics, the role-related patterns of alcohol use, the gender-related support for alcoholism treatment, and the denial of alcoholism as a problem requiring treatment are reinforced by a church view that alcoholism is a moral weakness. In general, these factors are responsible for the tendency of the Hispanic alcoholic family to enter treatment at a more advanced stage of alcoholism (Diaz, 1982; Rodriguez et al., 1979; Sierra, 1981). Gordon's study (1979) of Hispanic groups in a Northeast city and the Technical Systems Institute's study (1980) of three Hispanic communities in California both discovered a general reluctance to use the services that were available in the larger community.

Men have been the principal target group for alcoholism services, even though their families are reluctant to report alcohol-related problems to the appropriate caregivers. Gordon (1979) found that women are afraid to talk about their husbands to strangers in clinics or service institutions. To obtain help for their husbands or themselves, women are more likely to be in contact with a minister or a physician.

What role do the family and community play concerning the alcoholic? The cultural view of alcohol use and alcoholism indicates that different members of the family receive different kinds of help for alcohol-related problems from their families and from the community. Males receive more assistance from their families, who tend to attribute male alcohol abuse to external problems. Women receive little support and are directly blamed for their own alcohol abuse.

Some studies have indicated that the church's view of alcoholism as a moral weakness is a chief stumbling block in the way of outreach to Hispanic alcoholics and their families. In Gordon's study (1979) of the use of alcoholism services by Hispanics in one Northeastern United States city, Hispanics of different nationalities relied on the church as a helping institution. Both the Catholic Church and the Pentecostal Church were used by Hispanic alcoholics, although for different reasons, as supports to stop drinking. Diaz (1982) found that by working with the religious officials of the Pentecostal Church, support was developed for an education and treatment program for children of alcoholics. Once the church gave its approval to the program as consistent with its ideology, parents were willing to allow their children to attend cultural and educational activities at a youth center established in the church.

In general, research has found that Hispanics use intermediary indigenous or local services and institutions for help before going to traditional caregiver institutions. Certain characteristics of the indigenous institutions, such as ascribing respect and dignity to the male and maintaining a balance between the formality and informality of staff interactions with the Hispanic family, are cited as factors affecting this choice (Aguirrez, personal communication, March 1982; Rodriguez et al., 1979).

The family's refusal to consider itself as a client has affected the delivery of services to Hispanic children of alcoholics. Children receive mixed messages about treatment according to the sex of the alcoholic parent. Since the family does not typically enter treatment together, children are not involved in the rehabilitation process.

Hispanic children of alcoholics, like children of other cultural groups, need educational experiences that focus on the conflicts within their culture concerning alcohol use and alcoholism. This may be one way to educate parents and the extended family about the needs of the alcoholic as well. Culturally identifiable programs with bilingual staff may be the most successful way to reach the family as a whole. Although Hispanic professionals disagree about whether treating the whole family is a realistic goal, most agree that if the family is involved at some time, it will be beneficial for the recovery of the alcoholic member.

Black Americans

What functions does alcohol serve? Before black Africans were brought to the United States to work as servants and then as slaves, alcohol use was related to tribal and family celebrations and cere-monies. Many tribes made their own wine from vegetation that they cultivated. Although drinking was heavy during these ceremonial situations, behavior norms were established and alcohol use was not permitted to interfere with work. A great deal of social pressure was brought to bear on group members who abused drinking opportuni-ties and were unable to fulfill their roles as workers and providers for their families.

As servants and slaves in the United States, blacks were subject to control and restriction, including control of their use of alcohol. Different perspectives are expressed by black researchers on the participation of blacks in this control system. Some believe that slave owners gave alcohol to their slaves on holidays to control their behavior, keep them from running away, and keep them happy. Others believe that blacks were resourceful in convincing owners to provide this opportunity to socialize. This latter view holds that blacks created an innovative lifestyle for themselves that integrated their African heritage with an American one, combining music, dance, and drinking (Caldwell, 1981).

During the Civil War and Reconstruction periods, blacks in South-ern States were restricted from possessing both firearms and alco-hol. The fear that alcohol use would lead to uncontrolled revolt stemmed from concerns after the Nat Turner rebellion in 1830 (NIAAA, 1981d). These restrictions remained in effect after slaves won their freedom following the Civil War.

The migration of blacks to other areas in the United States to find work after the war resulted in the development of different drinking patterns. Away from their families, lacking money, and needing mutual support, blacks settled in the same areas, usually in poor housing that was readily available. Especially in the summer, people congregated outside to keep cool and to maintain friendships. Taverns fulfilled these social needs in the winter months. Drinking was a daily pastime for meeting friends and unwinding from jobs. On weekends, groups of friends drank inside and outside of taverns and on corners near their neighborhood stores and homes.

The pattern of group drinking continues among some socioeconomic groups, such as blue-collar workers and street people. Alcohol is used to stimulate conversation and social relationships. In general, blacks have been status-conscious drinkers, buying the more expensive name brands of liquor to impress their friends (Harper, 1976; NIAAA, 1981d).

How does the cultural group regard alcoholism? In the black community, alcoholism has been generally regarded as a moral weakness. This perspective stems from a cultural acceptance of certain intoxicated persons as permanent and less moral "characters" in the community, especially by the black churches. The church is a reference for moral standards and is often the center of family activities. Although the Protestant Church does not promote abstinence, it views alcoholism as a moral weakness that can be overcome by strengthened religious faith and activity. Some blacks belong to the Black Muslim religion which does require abstinence.

The view of alcoholism as a moral problem has prevented many black alcoholic families from seeking professional help. However, Wright (1981) reports that, once in treatment, black clients maintain their commitment to complete it.

Wheeler (1977) has identified other cultural issues affecting the black perspective on alcoholism. As a minority group in American society, blacks have frequently had to solve their own problems through the resources of their extended families or communities. Therefore, when drinking behavior interferes with family and work responsibilities, black families have turned to community networks of churches and social clubs for assistance. Some blacks perceive people who do seek the help of counselors as "sick." They are reluctant to use, and are less knowledgeable about, the services of psychology and psychiatry. This reluctance may also stem from the limited availability of culturally sensitive sources of treatment. Issues of confidentiality observed by members of these professions are also of great concern.

Harper (1976) reports that lack of knowledge about alcoholism and existing services in the black community partly reflects the lack of interest in alcoholism on the part of black leaders. These leaders have always focused on bringing issues of economic and social discrimination against blacks to the forefront of public discussion. Christmas (1978) observes that a similar preoccupation with living conditions has prevented chronic drinkers from identifying their own alcoholism as the problem. Even when rehabilitated through community detoxification programs, chronic drinkers do not demonstrate an interest to improve. They see the same conditions of life remaining in their community and they blame these conditions for their heavy drinking.

What roles do the family and community play concerning the alcoholic? Considering the cultural history of relying on family and community resources, these two human institutions should be an important part of any strategy to work with the black alcoholic. Blacks have not been consistent users of the existing social and health systems established by the white culture. Black researchers attribute this to inherent barriers of discrimination and insensitivity within these bureaucratic institutions.

Alcoholism specialists who have worked in the black community recommend that the alcoholic family would best be served by a comprehensive service program. Such a program would meet the variety of economic, social, and health needs of the family members. If all family members were participants in various programs at the same location, treatment of the whole family for the alcohol-related problems of one of its members could be coordinated within the service institution.

Black youths encounter stereotypical images of black alcoholics in the media and in daily community life. Researchers who assume that black youths are likely substance abusers compound the difficulty of combatting these images. Many black youths do not abuse alcohol or drugs. A more positive approach to involving black families in prevention and treatment programs is advocated by Crisp (1980).

Black children of alcoholics must confront the denial of alcoholism as a health problem and the negative self-image perpetuated in their own and majority communities. Crisp (1980) and Ortiz (1980) recommend developing education and prevention programs that first focus on the systemic problems of racism, sexism, power, and economic differences. Because many blacks see these problems as sources of frustration contributing to alcoholism, program developers identify a systemic focus as most effective in outreach efforts.

HOW DOES THE EXISTING HEALTH SYSTEM MEET THE NEEDS OF A VARIETY OF CLIENTS?

According to a report on mental health services for rural minorities (MITRE Corporation, 1981) and the articles by Christmas (1978), Davis (n.d.), and Harper (1976), the existing health service system of mental health centers, clinics, hospitals, and private treatment settings has a poor record of service for the minority client. Christmas reports that programs have been generally geared to the middle-aged, white male alcoholic who is recently employed and is at a low socioeconomic level. Historically, federal assistance in the development of alcoholism treatment programs has gone primarily to Native Americans (Christmas, 1978). Black treatment programs were supported originally through the Office of Economic Opportunity, when the prevailing theory held that economic and social discrimination were the cause of alcoholism in the black community. In the past decade, local affiliates have begun outreach efforts to minority communities. NIAAA has supported these efforts through materials developed by the National Center on Alcohol Education, the National Clearinghouse for Alcohol Information, and technical assistance for workshops.

Native Americans

At least through 1973, American Indian alcoholics were typically involved in three kinds of treatment programs: Alcoholics Anonymous; psychotherapy and psychiatry; and large-scale therapy with disulfiram, a drug creating a physical reaction to alcohol (Shore and Von Fumetti, 1972). These programs were established for the most part by non-Indians through the Office of Economic Opportunity and the Indian Health Service of the U.S. Public Health Service. All the authors reviewed here assert that programs should be developed and run by Indian tribal councils, that Indians should be recruited as staff, and that a program's philosophy of health should reflect the specific Indian group's definition of mental health. This policy has been adhered to by NIAAA in large-scale funding of Indian programs from 1973 to 1981.

Disparity between white and Indian philosophies of alcoholism and treatment and mistakes in staff training and assignment of responsibilities have hindered Native American program success in the past. These mistakes include hiring Indians just to give them jobs, hiring Indians believing that "Indianness" in itself is adequately therapeutic, and neglecting the training of Indian staff in the medical model and disease concept of alcoholism.

According to Miller and Ostendorf (1980), training of Indian counselors is well within the tradition of native healers and should not be slighted. To fulfill traditional roles in their tribes, native practitioners must undergo an apprenticeship and demonstrate their competence to their people. Miller and Ostendorf recommend that in white-sponsored health programs, Indian staff be hired who are stable, who "have a good heart," and who will not let family and tribal problems interfere with objective counseling. Although Indians are not always happy to be supervised by those from their own tribe, they will accept help more readily from Indians than from non-Indians.

Training should pay particular attention to the development of counseling skills. The confessional aspect of many counseling sessions of AA meetings is not consistent with Indian values of keeping personal information confidential or within one's family. Indian staff members must be able to convince their clients that confidentiality will be maintained even in these methods of treatment. Indian counselors trained in proven white health strategies will be able to explain what may seem like alien principles to their clients.

An important factor in program success is its perspective on the dimension of time. Indians value adequate time to make decisions and changes. In a white treatment program, this may be frustrating for the administrators and staff. A nontraditional scheduling approach is required to meet the needs of Indian clients. Hiring Indian counselors who understand this is one way to alleviate this potential source of tension (Wood, 1980; Miller and Ostendorf, 1980).

Family involvement in treatment must be approached cautiously. Males, who make up the largest percentage of alcoholics being treated in Indian programs, may not wish to talk about their lack of control of drinking in front of their wives and children. This factor may also affect the choice of a counselor assigned to work with the male alcoholic. Most prefer to talk with male peers as is consistent with the culturally valued social group experiences in which they learned to drink. In fact, recovered male alcoholic Indians have composed the staffs of most Indian alcoholism treatment programs until recently. As younger males and females are being educated in training programs like the one at the University of Utah and then hired by treatment programs, these older men have returned to other vocational opportunities on the reservation and in neighboring urban communities.

In a review of literature on Native Americans and alcoholism, Weibel (NIAAA, 1977) notes the lack of existing information on Native American women and alcoholism. Weibel reports reviewing more than 400 citations compiled in 1977 concerning alcoholism among Native Americans, not one of which specifically addressed the issues relevant to Native American women.

Some effects of alcoholism on Native American women have been reported, namely, (1) a high rate of fetal alcohol syndrome; (2) the high rate of cirrhosis deaths accounted for by females among Indians, almost half the total number of cirrhosis deaths; and (3) the neglect of children in alcoholic families (Ackerman, 1971; Malin et al., 1978; Streissguth, 1978). Differential drinking rates and rates of alcohol abuse have been noted by Weibel and Weisner (1980). The lack of research on drinking rates and the effects of alcoholism on women and their children has been deplored by Malin et al. (1978) and Leland (1978, 1980).

As do all counselors in the alcoholism field, Native American counselors receive a great deal of pressure from insurance companies and professional associations to obtain advanced training and degrees. This pressure is felt strongly by Indian counselors in white urban alcoholism programs that service Indians. For the most part, programs on the reservation serve people who do not carry health insurance; therefore, counselors working there are not as concerned with this credentialing movement (Wood, 1980).

Tribal council control of alcoholism programs can ensure the participation of the whole community in the mental health of its members. The establishment of nondrinking reference groups, the scheduling of drinking hours at Indian pubs, and the development of rules governing intoxicated pub customers and transportation of beer out of the pubs would demonstrate the tribe's ability to take action and combat the image of powerlessness and dependency that has stereotyped Native American people.

One example of an innovative response by a community to a concern for alcohol abuse is reported by Steinbring (1980) among the Saulteaux in Manitoba. When urban expansion brought easy access to alcohol, the community established AA as a symbol of unity against alcohol abuse. Membership in AA was a respected tradition; chapters were extensions of one's family group. Competition between chapters was active. Anonymity was given up to express pride in membership.

In this case a tribe applied Indian principles of family obligations to a white treatment method. Researchers working with Native Americans are still divided over which treatment and prevention strategies work best. Indians who are accultured do very well in white programs. For others, programs which incorporate Indian concepts of mental health seem more realistic. At the present time, defining the program goals with the Indian group designated as the target population, staffing and training it with Indian counselors, and institutionalizing it within the tribe are measures recommended by health providers working with Indian alcoholics.

Hispanic Americans

In general, the denial of alcohol problems by both Hispanics and service providers and the reluctance to use formal services for assistance result in an underutilization of human and health services by Hispanics. A majority of Hispanics do not consider alcoholism as a problem requiring treatment (Technical Systems Institute, 1980). The Hispanic alcoholic is generally identified upon presentation to traditional social and health institutions for treatment of alcohol-related medical, social, or economic problems.

Gordon (1979) found that these institutions lack consideration of cultural patterns of family interaction and alcohol use. Therefore, Hispanic women, the most likely group to present themselves and their families for assistance, are reluctant to use these traditional services. Women and children are the chief clients of community-based health centers. If community people are employed as aides and intake personnel, Gordon found that women are more willing to confide alcohol-related problems.

In a review of the use of service institutions in three California locales, the Technical Systems Institute (1980) found that a lack of communication between alcoholism and nonalcoholism agencies may have affected underutilization of services by Hispanics. Alcoholism service providers did not seem aware of other locally available services. Similarly, nonalcoholism services were not actively referring people to alcoholism services. Very few service providers directed their programs to Spanish-speaking subpopulations.

Black Americans

Wright (1981) reviewed the research literature on counseling blacks and found that it emphasizes an image of blacks as poor clients. Counseling the black client has been considered by many professionals to be counseling the culturally deprived. This notion was institutionalized by policy makers at the Federal and local levels through the use of terms such as "socially and culturally deprived" and "disadvantaged." Unfortunately, the stereotypes transmitted about the black client have prevented a genuine effort to understand the cultural differences inhibiting blacks from effectively using the existing services.

The structure and setting of alcoholism services are also factors in their underuse by blacks (Wright, 1981). Alcoholism services are traditionally not located within or near black communities. Blacks developed a pattern of choosing other alternatives to deal with their problems rather than trying to reach these and other medical and social services. When access to alcoholism programs was available, blacks found the structure and services limited. The treatment in these programs was therapeutic and focused on changing alcoholic behavior. Since blacks viewed other life circumstances as contributing factors in alcohol abuse, they preferred assistance for employment, housing, and nutrition needs. The lack of availability of these services and the lack of concern by those running the programs made participation in any other alcoholism services seem useless.

Another institutional barrier to the use of existing health services was the discrimination practiced by insurance companies. Insurance companies set rates based on actuarial tables indicating that blacks had a higher mortality rate than whites. Therefore, blacks were charged higher premiums. Of course, these policies made a difficult situation even worse. Traditionally, many blacks have been employed in jobs which do not provide health insurance and will not support individual purchases of policies. With increased costs incurred because of insurance projections, blacks were effectively discouraged from using services funded by third-party payments. A series of laws in 1935, 1943, and 1964 prohibited discrimination in insurance commission payments and premium charges and in writing, rating, or underwriting insurance policies.

Although the Office of Economic Opportunity supported the poverty alcoholism programs in the 1970s, black researchers report that services and trained alcoholism staff working in the black community are still inadequate. Black programs have problems in recruiting experienced and culturally sensitive staff and in becoming credentialed, as do other community-based programs for Native Americans and Hispanics. The recent formation of the National Black Alcoholism Council should give this cultural group a voice in State and Federal policies concerning prevention and treatment programs. Programs at Jackson State and Meharry Medical College provide opportunities to train black alcoholism professionals. The process of developing services to meet the needs of black alcoholics proceeds slowly. Meanwhile, practitioners advise the use of local community groups to publicize services, provide access to and information about insurance, and focus prevention efforts at young blacks still in the community.

SUMMARY

This review of cultural issues affecting service delivery has emphasized that cultural groups have histories of alcohol use that may or may not have an effect on the development of alcoholism in any one individual. However, the history and ways of responding to alcoholism do affect an alcoholic family's use of available health services.

There has been a poor service record in the delivery of services to meet the needs of cultural groups. Factors operating in this poor record are related to: (1) the structure of the service organization, (2) its staffing patterns, (3) its setting in relationship to the communities it serves, and (4) the attitudes toward alcoholism and health assistance held by the clients themselves. The following section examines these factors as professionals in the alcoholism field have analyzed them, in the hope of encouraging minority clients to use available services.

STAFFING, STRUCTURE, AND SETTING OF THE SERVICE

The practitioners reviewed here emphasize that to be successful in reaching diverse groups of clients, a program — whether educational or therapeutic — should include bilingual/bicultural staff and staff who have been trained to be sensitive to the needs of individual clients. Discriminatory hiring practices, the credentialing process, and the lack of specific training in minority health issues are cited as the crucial problems in hiring and retaining minority caregivers in professional positions.

In the alcoholism field there seem to be two perspectives on the staffing issue. Some practitioners argue that they cannot find certified minority caregivers to hire for their programs. A negative expectation seems to create a self-fulfilling prophecy; that is, very few minority caregivers are hired for professional roles, as opposed to nonprofessional and paraprofessional ones. As a result, minorities are less visible on the staff and their impact on the communities served is lessened considerably.

The other view is that the credentialing process supported by professional associations and insurance companies discriminates against the minority caregiver. Minorities argue that when treatment programs directed to minorities were first conceived, recovered alcoholics were hired to serve in professional roles. Community members recruited in the poverty alcoholism programs and in Indian reservation-based programs experimented with different outreach and treatment strategies that traditional agencies could not afford. Although nondegreed, these caregivers were providing the same services as specialists. When third-party payments became a critical funding source, insurance companies insisted on credentialed staff. Professionals graduating from degree programs joined in support of the establishment of national standards for alcoholism counselors and other caregivers.

As nondegreed caregivers try to attain these standards, they find their experience is discounted. They are required to enroll in summer alcoholism institutes or in university programs. Many find this too expensive and argue for credentials based on years and types of experience. Others recommend that insurance providers should be included on credentialing boards. The expectation is that an understanding of the job requirements and the overlapping job descriptions in alcoholism programs will lead to a more precise determination of the knowledge and skills required of different caregivers in a credentialed program.

All the researchers and practitioners cited in this chapter agree, however, that merely hiring minorities will not ensure effective service delivery to diverse groups of clients. Technical knowledge and sensitivity to cultural differences may be developed through training in specific courses in both summer institutes and university-sponsored inservice courses within agencies. Christmas (1978) recommends that staff at all levels understand the various blocks to accessing health systems, how individuals from different cultures perceive assistance from an institution, how different communication styles affect clinical experiences, and that negative experiences with bureaucracies are a part of almost all minority clients' past efforts to obtain health and social services.

Representation on boards of directors or advisory boards of diverse client groups is another important strategy to encourage usage by minority clients. Whether the setting is a community mental health center required to incorporate the views and needs of the communities it serves, a private hospital, or a social service agency, involvement in the policy-making of programs serves at least two purposes. By identifying and electing representatives of respected and powerful social and cultural groups within communities, community members are assured a voice in the policy decisions of the service agency. At the same time, minority board members take the message of service opportunities from the agency to their communities. Community members respect their leaders' involvement and are more likely to use the services on their recommendation. Hiring minority consultants and working with informal social networks such as churches and social clubs are two additional methods to disseminate service information and involve community members in service delivery.

The setting of a service agency can be a barrier to effective usage. Typically, the clients using social service agencies and clinics have less flexibility of time because of the kinds of jobs they hold and their job locations. Therefore, the establishment of a program in a work setting or within a minority community is more likely to encourage its use. The hours of the program operation and the flexibility of the staff are key components in a plan to encourage usage. In addition, linkages of staff, services, or locations of services with other agencies and hospitals will provide necessary support services for the clients and decrease the cost to one service agency of being all things to all clients. This is especially important when serving individuals who hold jobs without insurance benefits or who are unemployed.

CLIENT KNOWLEDGE AND ATTITUDES

Given the most supportive program and staff possible, the knowledge and attitudes of the clients are the motivating force in using available services. All the researchers and practitioners reviewed in this chapter have indicated that the clients' knowledge about alcohol and alcoholism, concern about the use of services outside the family and religious group, concern about payment for services, and identification of other problems as more serious prevent them from using alcoholism services.

Some cultural groups do not accept alcoholism as an illness and therefore do not view health services as an antidote to drinking. When alcoholism precipitates a crisis within the family, a loss of economic stability, a life-threatening situation, or trouble with the children, these clients are likely to turn to an institution or agency for help. At this point, the client is uninformed about payments or eligibility for financial assistance. The administrative procedures essential to the management of the agency are threatening and discourage clients from coming back and establishing a continuing, preventive relationship with the agency.

For these clients making a commitment to use services, a realization that the goals and strategies of a program conflict with their cultural views on family roles and religious beliefs may cause an interruption in program participation. Culturally recognizable caregivers and strategies, as indicated earlier, are essential to reassure clients that their perspectives are being incorporated in the program.

Most practitioners argue that community control of programs is the best strategy to ensure community use. The problems resulting from the community control perspective are related to the priorities held by the community and by local and State governments providing funding. Many cultural group leaders view unemployment as the cause of unrest and alcoholism. They are not interested in alcoholism programs focusing exclusively on the disease of alcoholism and would rather see a program established to deal with all the socioeconomic issues faced by community members, such as providing job training for recovered alcoholics as well as counseling for their families. They also view alcoholism and other mental health problems as employment opportunities for community members. With anticipated changes in the support of community programs, communities must examine their health and social needs and become involved in policymaking about social and health services.

Most prevention and treatment programs are developed, managed, and staffed by the nonindigenous culture. As a result, the values and attitudes figuring in an indigenous culture's response to alcoholism are generally not integrated into procedures and strategies. This may prevent people who most need the services from using what is available. Service institutions can alleviate the blocks to service use by the following strategies:

- Develop a program philosophy and goals with representatives of the client populations.
- Hire and train (both by inservice programs and by supporting enrollment in degree programs) staff from the client populations.
- Maintain documentation and evaluation systems to determine how well services are fulfilling community needs.
- Recruit community representatives for positions on advisory boards.
- Link services to community organizations and other service agencies.

GAPS IN SERVICES TO CULTURAL GROUPS

Researchers and practitioners concerned with delivery of services to alcoholic families of different cultures have made recommendations concerning filling the gaps in research, training of caregivers, and service programs.

The literature about alcoholics of different cultural groups reveals a lack of information on prevalence rates of alcoholism among subpopulations, family drinking patterns, and reasons for underutilization of existing services. Andrade (1980) and other researchers recommend that ethnic researchers be trained to conduct this work within their respective cultural groups.

A major concern of the authors reviewed in this chapter is for the training of alcoholism workers in bilingual/bicultural issues. The authors comment that, depending upon the degree of acceptance of the values of the majority culture among cultural groups, same-culture and different-culture caregivers are needed. Therefore, there has been an effort to develop materials for training both ethnic caregivers and majority culture caregivers to be aware of different perspectives held by caregivers and clients, and to be sensitive to the cultural identities of their clients. Some of these materials, such as the Cultural Family Assessment by Moore and Andrew and the Cultural and Ethnic Assessment Instruments by Silva, examine the cultural roles ascribed to individuals within a family and the issues they present for program planning. These culturally relevant materials have been developed chiefly for Hispanics and Native Americans. However, their principles of culture conflict and cultural identity assessment can be applied to any cultural group.

The lack of culturally specific programs is the major gap in delivery of services to cultural groups. This is especially true for children of alcoholics. A number of prevention/outreach programs have been established in minority communities to reach children and prevent them from using drugs or alcohol. However, Crisp (1980) and Ortiz (1980) maintain that many of these programs disregard the systemic issues that minorities see as the cause of their substance abuse problems. It does seem important to consider the problems of a community or cultural group as the starting point for program development, rather than imposing a particular model on all communities.

Each cultural group discussed in this chapter has particular needs to consider in the development of programs and training materials for caregivers. In general, not seeing alcoholism as a disease keeps many people from seeking help. This may actually be encouraged by religious beliefs, family customs, and cultural norms concerning handling the alcohol-related problems that would ordinarily bring families into contact with alcoholism specialists.

Cultural differences affect children of alcoholics in the following ways. Children receive mixed messages about the appropriate use of alcohol and about the recognition of alcoholism as a problem. They see men and women with alcohol problems treated differently in their families. This adds to confusion over understanding the illness of the alcoholic parent and compounds the problems generally associated with being a child of an alcoholic. There is little support for understanding these feelings and no support for getting help to deal with them.

In the vignette at the beginning of this chapter, the Southern Community Mental Health Center is making an effort to eliminate barriers to service delivery by hiring a minority consultant. While being responsive to the client populations they expect to serve, the staff at this center can also turn their attention to the children of these families.

All the information reported in this chapter indicates that children in the cultural groups addressed are prime audiences for prevention and education programs.

Chapter V

Summary and Recommendations

We are aware that in making the following recommendations, it is unlikely that substance abuse among the families of preschool children will ever be eradicated. However, it can be reduced significantly. To do so, we must begin to think of substance abuse in a community and societal context, rather than in an individual context. To think of substance abuse as an individual problem in effect blames the individual for its occurrence. "Blaming the Victim" (Ryan, 1971) is done frequently in society, on a range of other social problems other than substance abuse. We must also think of local community involvement, rather than always of what large governmental bodies can "do" to solve the problem. Native American substance abuse represents a massive social problem (Lobb and Watts, 1989; Mail and McDonald, 1980) and it has been proposed by Beauvais and LaBoueff (1985) and Watts and Lewis (1988) that the local community be involved in a dynamic way in resolving the problem.

Substance abuse always occurs in a cultural, social, and economic context. It cannot be looked at outside the specific cultural locations in which it happens (Helmer, 1975; Watts, 1986). That cultural location or context could be Afro-American (Watts and Wright, 1983), Native American (Weibel-Orlando, 1984; Williams, 1985; Indian Health Service, 1977), Hispanic American (Gilbert, 1989; Mayers et al., forthcoming), or other ethnic groups. The cultural context of social problems and the human services in general is all-important (Wright et al., 1983). It is anchored in a socioeconomic context (Nusbaumer, 1983). To a low-income minority youth caught in a ghetto or barrio, substance abuse may represent (at the time) a temporary escape. Substance abuse policies that only look at the individual actions of the person consuming and abusing a given substance, and not at the total environment (grinding poverty and deprivation, unrelieved stress, etc.) are doomed to fail. The following recommendations are worthy of consideration:

1. Increase child-care services within substance abuse treatment programs. If a female single parent of a preschooler is a substance abuser and needs treatment, then some kind of child-care service must be available while she is in treatment unless she is fortunate to have relatives or close friends to care for her child.

2. Fetal alcohol syndrome must be a priority item on the policy agenda. Efforts need to be made in particular with the Native Americans, who are especially affected. Minority women also are more affected than white women. FAS prevention should focus on segmenting high-risk populations. FAS prevention messages should be directed at younger populations of women as part of school-based substance abuse education. Again, environments must be studied and dealt with. A Sioux Native American woman in South Dakota in an economically depressed region experiences little hope of climbing out of that environment. FAS prevention programs must recognize the total environment (poverty, etc.).

3. More research is needed on the long-term effects of intrauterine exposure to drugs. This research is needed in respect to implementing effective prevention and treatment efforts.

4. Early identification of substance abuse problems must be made in maternal and infant service delivery systems. Staff need to be sensitized to the existence of substance abuse problems. After identification of substance abuse problems in these programs, prevention and intervention efforts must be effected as soon as possible.

5. Identify preschool children of substance-abusing parents in demographic studies including household surveys, high school senior surveys, and through other statistics. Research grants need to be directed toward programs that identify and treat this population. Based on the success of Head Start programs, this is the most likely point of effective intervention to prevent substance abuse in the future. Related to this, parental consent vs. children's rights to be protected need to be thoroughly explored and policy decisions made to clarify these issues.

6. Programs that address this population should be encouraged with research money to establish effective treatment and evaluation strategies that account for the developmental cognitive ability of these children.

7. All drug and alcohol treatment programs should have a segment for the significant family members of the substance abuser in treatment based on a structural family system model or an effective parent or family skills training program. If the program is unable to engage the family in the treatment process, then the treatment community and the AA or NA recovering community can become the family for the recovering addict. It is highly likely that without drug free support an addict or alcoholic will relapse.

8. Prevention and early intervention in respect to child bearing-age women must be made a priority. Suspected teratological substances must be identified and this information disseminated. Pregnancy health promotion programs must replace scare campaigns.

9. Extensive drug and alcohol histories including intergenerational history should be taken on all pregnant women or anyone treated for a substance related illness in a hospital setting.

10. Community-based programs should be formed by members of that community to assure an ethnic or socioeconomic sensitivity and appropriateness.

11. Staff at existing institutions and agencies who address issues often correlated with substance abuse should have training in substance abuse, i.e., child protective services, Head Start, teachers, social workers, physicians.

12. Research with a systems approach that views families, communities, and impact of information (media) as interactive components instead of separate entities should be encouraged.

13. Health care providers' educational requirements in substance abuse should be standardized and a prevention model of wellness/health promotion should be advocated.

14. Outreach to specific populations should be considered on the basis of proportion of substance abuse in a given population compared to the norm and the underrepresentation of that population in treatment. High on the list would be women and minorities.

15. More research-based substance abuse education programs for youth are needed. We emphasize the words "research-based" be-

cause many programs have not been adequately researched. Especially needed are long-term, follow-up studies to see if these programs make a difference.

16. The role of the Public Health Service fostered under the current C.E.O., should continue in taking a proactive stance in the area of prevention and disseminating information on AIDS, FAS, and the use/abuse of licit (alcohol, tobacco) and illicit drugs (cocaine/crack, PCP, heroin, marijuana, etc.).

17. Insurance coverage for chemical dependency treatment should be mandated to provide the necessary economic environment in which treatment effectiveness would have to be demonstrated, or programs would not be covered.

18. The medical profession must clarify its contribution to the chemical dependency field and foster policy-making that will clarify this position to insurers, patients, and other professions. The American Medical Association has taken definitive stances on policies concerning smoking and other health problems that bode well in this regard.

19. Public policy should be based on a public health model of substance abuse and addiction. There should be a reduced emphasis and spending on legal, moralistic approaches.

20. Substance abuse policies should include large-scale social welfare initiatives. One of the best ways to conduct a "war on drugs" (if we must use the "war" analogy) would be to conduct a war on poverty, inequality, illiteracy, and other social ills. Goodman (1989:3) notes that what we need "is less of an assault mentality and more of a healing one."

The challenge for policy makers, administrators, researchers, and providers is to recognize the holistic approach to prevention and treatment and to implement some of the prevention and intervention strategies addressed in this book if we are to turn the corner on this devastating disease that is damaging so many preschool children and their families.

Chapter VI

References

Abel, E. (1985). Effects of prenatal exposure to cannabinoids. In T. Pinkert (Ed.), *Consequences of Maternal Drug Abuse* [Research Monograph], 59, 48-60. Rockville, MD: National Institute of Drug Abuse.

Ackerman, L. A. (1971). Marital instability and juvenile delinquency among the Nez Perces. *American Anthropologist*, 73(3), pp. 595-603.

Adler, R., & Raphael B. (1983). Children of alcoholics [Review]. *Australian and New Zealand Journal of Psychiatry*, 17, 3-8.

Alcohol, Drug Abuse, and Mental Health News (1984, January). Young children of alcoholics target of prevention program, 10(1). Author.

Alcoholics Anonymous. (1939). New York: Alcoholics Anonymous World Services, Inc.

Andrade, S. J. (1980). Intercultural Development Research Association Newsletter of the Mental Health Research Project. *Mexican American Women and Social Science Research*, 2(2).

Bacon, S. (1987). Alcohol problem prevention: A common sense approach. *Journal of Drug Issues*, 17(4), 369-393.

Bandy, P., & President, P. (1983). Recent literature on drug abuse prevention and mass media: Focusing on youth, parents, women, and the elderly. *Journal of Drug Education*, 13(3), 255-271.

Bartunek. (1982). Minimal interventions designed to generate systemic change: An overview and an example taken from a large corporate system intervention. In W. Gray, J. Fidler, & J. Battista (Eds.), *General Systems Theory and the Psychological Sciences*, (Vol. 1), (pp. 139-145).

Battjes, R. J., & Bell, C. S. (1985). Future directions in drug abuse prevention research. In C. S. Bell, & R. Battjes (Eds.), *Prevention Research: Deterring Drug Abuse Among Children and Adolescents* (pp. 221-228). Rockville, MD: National Institute on Drug Abuse.

Baumrind, D. (1985). Familial antecedents of adolescent drug use: A developmental perspective. In C. L. Jones & R. J. Battjes (Eds.), *Etiology of Drug Abuse: Implications for Prevention* [Research Monograph], 56, 13-44. Rockville, MD: National Institute of Drug Abuse.

Bean-Bayog, M. (1987). Children of alcoholics [Guest Editorial]. *Advances in Alcohol and Substance Abuse, 6*(4), 1-2.

Beauchamp, D. (1976). Alcoholism as blaming the alcoholic. *The International Journal of the Addictions, 11*(1), 41-52.

Beauvais, F., and LaBoueff, S. (1985, January). Drug and alcohol abuse intervention in American Indian communities. *The International Journal of the Addictions, 20*(1), 139-171.

Bell, C., & Battjes, R. (1985). Overview of drug abuse prevention research. In C. S. Bell, & R. Battjes (Eds.), *Prevention Research: Deterring Drug Abuse Among Children and Adolescents* [Research Monograph], 63, 1-7. Rockville, MD: National Institute on Drug Abuse.

Bell, W. (1987). *Contemporary social welfare*, (2nd ed.). New York: Macmillan Publ. Co.

Bepko, C. (1984). *The responsibility trap: A blueprint for treating the alcoholic family*. Berkeley, CA: Free Press.

Bepko, C. (1988). Female legacies: Intergenerational themes and their treatment for women in alcoholic families. *Journal of Psychotherapy and the Family, 3*(4), 97-111.

Black, C., Bucky, S., & Wilder-Padilla, S. (1986). The interpersonal and emotional consequences of being an adult child of an alcoholic. *The International Journal of the Addictions, 21*(2), 213-231.

Black, R. Mayer, J., & MacDonall, J. (1981). Child abuse and neglect in families with an opiate addicted parent. In T. J. Glynn (Ed.), *Drugs and the Family*, (pp. 74-76). Rockville, MD: National Institute on Drug Abuse.

Blinick, G., Tovolga, W., & Antopol, W. (1977). Variations in birth cries of newborn infants from narcotic-addicted and normal mothers. In P. Ferguson, T. Lennox, & D. Lettieri (Eds.), *Drugs and Pregnancy* [Research Issues], *5*, 77-79. Rockville, MD: National Institute on Drug Abuse.

Blum, R. (1980). An argument for family research. In B. G. Ellis (Ed.), *Drug Abuse from the Family Perspective*. Rockville, MD: National Institute on Drug Abuse.

Blum, R., et al. (1972). *Horatio Alger's children: The role of the family in the origin and prevention of drug abuse*. San Francisco: Jossey-Bass.

Blume, S. (1987). Public policy issues relevant to children of alcoholics. *Advances in Alcohol and Substance Abuse*, *6*(4), 1-15.

Botvin, G., & Wills, T. (1985). Personal and social skills training; cognitive-behavioral approaches to substance abuse prevention. In C. S. Bell, & R. Battjes (Eds.), *Prevention Research: Deterring Drug Abuse Among Children and Adolescents* [Research Monograph], *63*, 8-49. Rockville, MD: National Institute of Drug Abuse.

Braucht, G. N., & Braucht, B. (1984). Prevention of problem drinking among youth: Evaluation of educational strategies. In P. M. Miller & T. D. Nirenberg (Eds.), *Prevention of Alcohol Abuse* (pp. 253-279). New York: Plenum Press.

Brisbane, F. L. (1985). Using contemporary fiction with black children and adolescents in alcoholism treatment. In F. L. Brisbane and M. Womble (Eds.), *Treatment of Black Alcoholics* (pp. 179-197). New York: Haworth Press.

Burgess, R., & Richardson, R. (1984). Coercive interpersonal contingencies as a determinant of child maltreatment: Implications for treatment and prevention. In R. F. Dangel & R. A. Polster (Eds.), *Parent Training: Foundations of Research and Practice* (pp. 239-257). New York: Guilford Press.

Bush, P., & Iannotti, R. (1985). The development of children's health orientations and behaviors: Lessons for substance use prevention. In C. L. Jones, & R. J. Battjes (Eds.), *Etiology of Drug Abuse: Implications for Prevention* [Research Monograph], *56*, 13-44. Rockville, MD: National Institute of Drug Abuse.

Caldwell, F. J. (1981). "Alcoholics Anonymous as a viable treatment resource for black alcoholics." Paper presented at NIAAA

Workshop, Rockville, MD: National Institute on Alcohol Abuse and Alcoholism.

Chambers, C. D., & Hart, L. G. (1977). Drug use patterns in pregnant women. In J. L. Rementeria (Ed.), *Drug Abuse in Pregnancy and Neonatal Effects*. St. Louis: Mosby.

Children's Defense Fund. (1988). *What every American should be asking political leaders in 1988*. Washington, DC.

Christmas, J. J. (1978, Spring). Alcoholism services for minorities: Training issues and concerns. *Alcohol Health and Research World*.

Clayton, R., Voss, H., Robbins, C., & Skinner, W. (1986). Gender differences in drug use: An epidemiological perspective. In B. Ray, & M. Braude (Eds.), *Women and Drugs: A New Era in Research* [Research Monograph], *65*, 80-99. Rockville, MD: National Institute on Drug Abuse.

Coleman, S. (1981). Incomplete mourning in substance abusing families: Theory, research, and practice. In T. J. Glynn (Ed.), *Drugs and the Family*. Rockville, MD: National Institute on Drug Abuse.

Coleman, S., & Stanton, M. D. (1981). The role of death in the addict family. In T. J. Glynn (Ed.), *Drugs and the Family*. Rockville, MD: National Institute on Drug Abuse.

Cooley, R. (1980). Alcoholism programs for Native Americans. In J. Waddell, & M. Everett (Eds.), *Drinking Behavior Among Southwestern Indians*, pp. 205-213. Tucson: University of Arizona Press.

Crisp, A. D. (1980, January-March). Making substance abuse prevention relevant to low-income black neighborhoods. *Journal of Psychedelic Drugs*, *12*(1).

The Dallas Morning News (June 29, 1989). Cocaine used in childbirth, pg. 8a.

Davis, Jr., T. (not dated). *Alcoholism: Needs of Minorities*. New York: National Council on Alcoholism.

DeMarsh, J., & Kumpfer, K. (1986, Fall/Winter). Family oriented interventions for the prevention of chemical dependency in children and adolescents. *Children in Contemporary Society*, *18* (1-2), 117-151.

Densen-Gerber, J., & Rohrs, C. (1981). Drug addicted parents and child abuse. *Contemporary Drug Problems*, 2(4), 683-696.

Diaz, P. (1982, April). "Reaching Hispanic Children of Alcoholics in Their Own Community." Paper presented at the National Council on Alcoholism Annual Forum, Washington, DC.

Doering, P. L., & Stewart, R. B. (1978). The extent and character of drug consumption during pregnancy. *JAMA*, *239*, 843-846.

Editorial Research Reports. (1985). *Education report card: Schools on the line*. Washington, DC.

Edwards, D. (1982, Spring). Spouse participation in the treatment of alcoholism: Completion of treatment and recidivism. *Social Work with Groups*, *5*(1), 41-48.

Edwards, D., & Zander, T. (1985, December). Children of alcoholics: Background and strategies for the counselor. *Elementary School Guidance and Counseling*, *20*(2), 121-128.

Ellis, B. (1980). Report of a workshop on reinforcing the family system as the major resource in the primary prevention of drug abuse. In B. G. Ellis (Ed.), *Drug Abuse from the Family Perspective: Coping is a Family Affair*. Rockville, MD: National Institute on Drug Abuse.

Escalante, F. (1980). Group pressure and excessive drinking among Native Americans. In J. Waddell, & M. Everett (Eds.), *Drinking Behavior Among Southwestern Indians*, pp. 183-204. Tucson: University of Arizona Press.

Ferguson, F. N. (1976). Stake theory as an explanatory device in Navajo alcoholism treatment response. *Human Organization*, *35*(1), pp. 65-78.

Finnegan, L. P. (1983). Clinical, perinatal and developmental effects of methodone. In J. R. Cooper, F. Altman, B. S. Brown, & D. Czechowicz (Eds.), *Research on the Treatment of Narcotic Addiction: State of the Art*. National Institute on Drug Abuse [Monograph], (DHHS Pub. No. ADM 83-1281) (pp. 392-443). Washington, DC: Supt. of Docs., U.S. Gov. Print Off.

Finnegan, L., Connaughton, J., Emich, J., et al. (1977). Comprehensive care of the pregnant addict and its effect on maternal and infant outcome. In T. Pinkert (Ed.), *Consequences of Maternal Drug Abuse* [Research Monograph], *59*, 48-60. Rockville, MD: National Institute on Drug Abuse.

Forfar, J. O., & Nelson, M. N. (1973). Epidemiology of drugs taken by pregnant women: Drugs that may effect the fetus adversely. *Clin Pharmacalther*, *14*, 632-642.

Fort Worth Star Telegram. Fort Worth, Texas. (1989, July 2, Sunday). p. 9.

French, S. (1987). Family approaches to alcoholism: Why the lack of interest among marriage and family therapists? *Journal of Drug Issues*, *17*(4), 359-368.

Fried, P. (1985). Postnatal consequences of maternal marijuana use. In T. Pinkert (Ed.), *Consequences of Maternal Abuse* [Research Monograph] *59*, 48-60. Rockville, MD: National Institute on Drug Abuse.

Fried, P. A., Innes, K. S., & Barnes, M. V. (1984). Soft drug use prior to and during pregnancy: A comparison of samples over a four-year period. *Drug Alcohol Depend*, *13*, 161-176.

Gibson, G. T., Baghurst, P. A., & Colley, D. P. (1983). Maternal alcohol, tobacco and cannabis consumption and the outcome of pregnancy. *AUST NZ J. Obstet Gynaec*, *23*, 15-19.

Gilbert, M. J. (1989). Hispanic Americans: Alcohol use, abuse and adverse consequences. In T. D. Watts and R. Wright, Jr. (Eds.), *Alcoholism in Minority Populations*, (pp. 55-75). Springfield, IL: Charles C Thomas Publ. Also see: Delgado, M. (1989). Treatment and prevention of Hispanic alcoholism. In T. D. Watts and R. Wright, Jr. (Eds.), *Alcoholism in Minority Populations* (pp. 77-92). Springfield, IL: Charles C Thomas Publ.

Globetti, G. (1989). Alcohol prevention programs and minorities. In T. D. Watts, & R. Wright, Jr. (Eds.), *Alcoholism in Minority Populations* (pp. 191-211). Springfield, IL: Charles C Thomas Publ.

Gordon, A. J. (1979). Cultural and organizational factors in the delivery of alcohol treatment services to Hispanics. *Working Papers on Alcohol and Human Behavior*, No. 7. Providence, RI: Brown University, Department of Anthropology.

Greenspan, S. (1985). Research strategies to identify developmental vulnerabilities for drug abuse. In C. L. Jones, & R. J. Battjes (Eds.), *Etiology of Drug Abuse: Implications for Prevention* [Research Monograph], *56*, 13-44. Rockville, MD: National Institute on Drug Abuse.

Hahn, A., Danzberger, J., & Lefkowitz, B. (1987). *Dropouts in America: Enough is known for action.* Washington, DC: Institute for Educational Leadership.

Harper, F. D. (Ed.). (1976). *Alcohol abuse and black America.* Alexandria, VA: Douglass Publishers.

Hawkins, D., Lishner, D., & Catalano, R. (1985). Childhood predictors and the prevention of adolescent substance abuse. In C. L. Jones, & R. J. Battjes (Eds.), *Etiology of Drug Abuse: Implications for Prevention* [Research Monograph], *56*, 13-44. Rockville, MD: National Institute on Drug Abuse.

Hazelden Professional Update. (March, 1989). Model prevention program in Chicago County, Minnesota, is paying off, *7*(3). Author.

Hecht, M. (1973, October). Children of alcoholics are children at risk. *American Journal of Nursing, 73*(10).

Helmer, J. (1975). *Drugs and minority oppression.* New York: The Seabury Press.

Henderson, C. (1985). Countering resistance to acceptance of denial and the disease concept in alcoholic families: Two examples of experiential teaching. *Alcoholism Treatment Quarterly, 1*(4), 117-121.

Hill, R. M. (1973). Drugs ingested by pregnant women. *Clin Pharmacy Therapeutics, 14*, 654-659.

Hingson, R., Gould, J. B., Morelock, S., Kayne, H., Heeron, T., Alpert, J. J., Zuckerman, B., & Day, N. (1982). Maternal cigarette smoking, psychoactive substance use, and infant apgar scores. *Obstet Gynocol, 144*, 259-266.

Indian Health Service. (1977). *Alcoholism: A high priority health problem.* A report of the Indian Health Service Task Force on Alcoholism (DHEW Pub. No. HSA 77-1001). Washington, DC: Indian Health Service.

Johnson, J., & Bennet, L. (1988). *School-aged children of alcoholics: Theory and research.* New Brunswick, NJ: Alcohol Research Documentation, Inc., Rutgers University.

Kadushin, A., & Martin, J. (1981). *Child abuse: An interactional event.* New York: Columbia University Press.

Kahn, E., Neumann, L., & Polk, G. (1977). The course of the heroin withdrawal syndrome in newborn infants treated with phenobarbital or chlorpromazine. In P. Ferguson, T. Lennox, and D. Lettieri (Eds.), *Drugs and Pregnancy*. Rockville, MD: National Institute on Drug Abuse.

Kandall, S. R., Albin, S., Gartner, L. M., Leek, S., Eidelman, A., & Lowman, J. (1979). The narcotic dependent mother: Fetal and neonatal consequences. *Early Human Development*, *1*(2), 159.

Kaslow, F. (1980). The strata beneath the presenting problem. In B. G. Ellis (Ed.), *Drug Abuse from the Family Perspective* (DHHS Publication No. ADM 80-910). Rockville, MD: National Institute on Drug Abuse.

Kenward, K., & Rissover, J. (1980). A family systems approach to the treatment and prevention of alcoholism: A review. *Family Therapy*, *7*(2), 97-106.

Kinder, B., Pape, N., & Walfish, S. (1980). Drug and alcohol education programs: A review of outcome studies. *The International Journal of the Addictions*, *15*(7), 1035-1054. In T. Glynn (Ed.), *Drug Abuse Prevention Research* [Research Issues], *33*. Rockville, MD: National Institute on Drug Abuse.

Kolata, G. (1989, July 19). A new toll of alcohol abuse: The Indians' next generation. *New York Times*, pp. 1, 10.

Landesman-Dwyer, S. (1982). Maternal drinking and pregnancy outcome. *Applied Research In Mental Retardation*, *3*, 241-263.

Landress, H. (1983). School based prevention programs for potential drug abusers. *Social Work in Education*, *5*(4), 241-257.

Leland, J. (1978). Women and alcohol in an Indian settlement. *Medical Anthropologist*, *2*(4), pp. 85-119.

Leland, J. (1980). Native American alcohol use, a review of the literature. In P. D. Mail, & D. R. McDonald, (Eds.), *Tulapai to Tokay: A Bibliography of Alcohol Use and Abuse Among Native Americans of North America*. New Haven: Human Relations Area Files.

Lifschitz, M. H., Wilson, G. S., O'Brian, J., Faneth, E., & Desmond, M. M. (1983). Fetal and postnatal growth of children born to narcotic dependent women. *J. Pediatr*, *102*, 646.

Lindesmith, A. (1982). The federal narcotics bureaucracy and drug policy. In T. J. Glynn, & J. E. Nelson (Eds.), *Public Health Issues and Drug Abuse Research* [Research Issue], *30*. Rockville, MD: National Institute on Drug Abuse.

Linn, S., Schoenbaum, S. C., Monson, R. R., Rosner, R., Stubblefield, P. C., & Rayn, K. J. (1983). The association of marijuana with outcomes of pregnancy. *Am Public Health, 73,* 1161-1164.

Lobb, M. L., & Watts, T. D. (Eds.) (1989). *Native American youth and alcohol: An annotated bibliography.* Westport, CT: Greenwood Press. Also, see Lobb, M. L. & Watts, T. D., Native American youth and alcohol. *Akwesasne Notes, 22*(3), Summer, 1990, pp. 18-25. Reprinted from the book.

Lutzker, J. (1984). A review of project 12-ways: An ecobehavioral approach to the treatment and prevention of child abuse and neglect. *Advances in Behavior Research Therapy, 6,* 63-73.

Lutzker, J. (1984). Project 12-ways: Treating child abuse and neglect from an ecobehavioral perspective. In R. F. Dangel, & R. A. Polster (Eds.), *Parent Training: Foundations of Research and Practice* (pp. 260-295). New York: Guilford Press.

Mail, P. D., & McDonald, D. R. (Comps.) (1980). *Tulapai to Tokay: A bibliography of alcohol use and abuse among Native Americans of North America.* New Haven, CT: HRAF Press. Also, see P. A. May (1989). Alcohol abuse and alcoholism among Native Americans: An overview. In T. D. Watts and R. Wright, Jr. (Eds.), *Alcoholism in Minority Populations,* (pp. 95-119). Springfield, IL: Charles C Thomas Publ.

Malin, H. J., Munch, N. E., & Archer, L. D. (1978). *A National Surveillance System for Alcoholism and Alcohol Abuse.* Report to 32nd International Congress on Alcoholism and Drug Dependence. Rockville, MD: National Institute on alcohol Abuse and Alcoholism.

Manning, D. (1987). Books as therapy for children of alcoholics. *Child Welfare, 66*(1), 35-43.

Mason, V., & Baker, G. (1978). *Growing up and feeling powerful as an American Indian.* Rockville, MD: National Institute on Drug Abuse.

Mason, V. G. (1982, April). "Reaching the Native American children of alcoholic families." Papers presented at the National Council on Alcoholism Annual Forum, Washington, DC.

May, P., & Hambaugh, K. (1982). A pilot project in fetal alcohol syndrome among American Indians. *Alcohol Health and Research World*, 7(2), 3-9.

Mayers, R.S., Kail, B.L., & Watts, T. (forthcoming). *Hispanic Substance Abuse*. Springfield, IL: Charles C Thomas, Publ.

McKenna, T., & Pickens, R. (1981). Alcoholic children of alcoholics. *Journal of Studies on Alcohol*, 42(11), 1021-1029.

McKelvey v. Turnage, 86 S. Ct. 737 (1988).

Miller, M., & Ostendorf, D. (1980). Mental health programs. In J. Waddell, & M. Everett (Eds.), *Drinking Behavior Among Southwestern Indians*. Tucson: University of Arizona Press.

MITRE Corporation (1981). *Mental health services for rural minorities*. Research and Development Center for Rural Mental Health, National Institute of Mental Health.

Moos, R., & Billings, R. (1982). Children of alcoholics during the recovery process: Alcoholic and matched control families. *Addictive Behaviors*, 7, 155-163.

Mullen, P. (1983, February). Promoting child health: Channels of socialization. *Family and Community Health* (pp. 52-68).

Naiditch, B. (1986). Why work with children of alcoholics? In R. Ackerman (Ed.), *Growing in the Shadow: Children of Alcoholics* (pp. 87-90).

Naiditch, B. (1988, Summer). Rekindled spirit of a child: Intervention strategies for shame with elementary age children of alcoholics. *Alcoholism Treatment Quarterly*, 4(2), 57-69.

Nathenson, G., Golden, G., & Litt, I. (1976). Diazepam in the management of the neonatal narcotic withdrawal syndrome. In P. Ferguson, T. Lennox, & D. Letticri (Eds.), *Drugs and Pregnancy*. Rockville, MD: National Institute on Drug Abuse.

National Council on Alcoholism. (1980, June). *A position paper on alcoholism and minorities*. New York: The Council.

National Institute on Alcohol Abuse and Alcoholism. (1983). *Prevention plus: Involving schools, parents, and the community in alcohol and drug education* (DHHS Publication No. ADM83-1256). Rockville, MD: Author.

National Institute on Alcohol Abuse and Alcoholism (1977). American Indians, urbanization, and alcohol: A developing urban Indian drinking ethos, by J. C. Weibel. In, *Special Population Is-*

sues. Alcohol and Health Monograph No. 4. Washington, DC: Supt. of Docs., U.S. Gov't. Print. Off., pp. 331-358.

National Institute on Alcohol Abuse and Alcoholism. (1980a, August), Alcohol and American Indians. *Alcohol Topics in Brief*. Rockville, MD: National Clearinghouse for Alcohol Information.

National Institute on Alcohol Abuse and Alcoholism. (1981d). Skills development workshop. "Self-Definition, Self-Determination, Self-Solution: Agenda for Black Alcoholism Programs." Jackson State University, Jackson, MS.

National Institute on Alcohol Abuse and Alcoholism. (1987). *Program strategies for preventing fetal alcohol syndrome and alcohol related birth defects*. Rockville, MD: Author.

National Institute on Alcohol Abuse and Alcoholism. (1987). *Sixth special report to the U.S. Congress on alcohol and health*. Rockville, MD: Author.

National Institute on Drug Abuse. (1977). *Indian in the red: A reality or a myth?* DHHS Pub. No. (ADM) 81-492. Washington, DC: Supt. of Docs., U.S. Gov't. Print. Off.

National Institute on Drug Abuse (1986). *A guide to mobilizing ethnic minority communities for drug abuse prevention* (DHHS Publication No. ADM 86-1465). Rockville, MD: Author.

National Institute on Drug Abuse. (1987). *Drug abuse and drug abuse research*. Rockville, MD: Author.

Nusbaumer, M. R. (1983, April 28-30). Alcohol, social control, and the disease of alcoholism: A critical analysis. Paper delivered at the North Central Sociological Association Annual Meeting.

Ortiz, C. (1980, January-March). In, A. Crisp (Ed.), Making substance abuse prevention relevant to low-income black neighborhoods. *Journal of Psychedelic Drugs*, *12*(1).

Panel Workshop: Violence, crime, sexual abuse and addiction. *Contemporary Drug Problems*, *5*(3), 385-440, 1976.

Parachini, A. (1981, June 21). The cantina culture. *This World*.

Pokorny, A. (1980). Report on a national survey; results of the survey. In M. Galanter (Ed.), *Alcohol and Drug Abuse in Medical Education*. Rockville, MD: National Institute on Drug Abuse.

Rementeria, J., & Nunag, N. (1973). Narcotic withdrawal in pregnancy: Stillbirth incidence with a case report. In P. Ferguson, T. Lennox, and D. Lettieri (Eds.), *Drugs and Pregnancy*. Rockville, MD: National Institute on Drug Abuse.

Resnick, H. (1980). *Drug abuse prevention for low-income communities: Manual for Program Planning*. Rockville, MD: National Institute on Drug Abuse.

Rodriguez, L., Morgan, D., & Rodriguez, A. (1979). Therapeutic involvement of the family in treating Hispanic alcoholics: Two Miami programs.

Romero, L. (not dated). *La Mujer: The Mexican American alcoholic woman – who is she?* Harlingen, TX: RGV Midway House.

Rothberg, N. (1986, Spring). The alcoholic spouse and the dynamics of co-dependency. *Alcoholism Treatment Quarterly*, *3*(1), 73-86.

Ryan, W. (1971). *Blaming the Victim*. New York: Pantheon.

Sanchez-Dirks, R. (1978/79, Winter). Drinking patterns among Hispanic youth. *Alcohol Health and Research World*.

Satir, V. (1967). Family systems and approaches to family therapy. *Journal of the Fort Logan Mental Health Center*, *4*, 81-93.

Scavnicky-Mylant, M. (1984, August). Children of alcoholics: Children in need. *Family and Community Health*, *7*(2), 51-62.

Schulman, C. (1977). Alterations of the sleep cycle in heroin-addicted and "suspect" newborns. In P. Ferguson, T. Lennox, and D. Lettieri (Eds.), *Drugs and Pregnancy*. Rockville, MD: National Institute on Drug Abuse.

Segal, B. (1986). Intervention and prevention of drug-taking behavior: A need for divergent approaches. *The International Journal of the Addictions*, *21*, 165-173.

Shore, J., & Von Fumetti, B. (1972). Three alcohol programs for American Indians. *American Journal of Psychiatry*, *128*, p. 11.

Sierra, J. (1981, April). "The minority family with alcoholism." Paper presented at the National Council on Alcoholism Annual Forum, New Orleans.

Sokol, R. J., Miller, S. I., & Reed G. (1980). Alcohol abuse during pregnancy: An epidemiologic study. *Alcohol: Clin Exper. Res.*, *4*, 137-145.

Stanton, M. (1980). Some overlooked aspects of the family and drug abuse. In B. Ellis (Ed.), *Drug Abuse from the Family Per-*

spective: Coping is a Family Affair (DHHS Publication NO. 80-910). Rockville, MD: National Institute on Drug Abuse.

Stanton, M., Todd, T., Steier, F., Van Deusen, J. M., Marder, L. R., Rosoff, R., Seaman, S., & Skibinski, E. (1979). Family characteristics and family therapy of heroin addicts: Final report 1974-1978. In T. Glynn (Ed.), *Drugs and the Family* (DHHS Publication No. ADM 81-1151). Rockville, MD: National Institute on Drug Abuse.

Steinbring. (1980). In J. Waddell & M. Everett (Eds), *Drinking Behavior Among Southwestern Indians*. Tucson: University of Arizona Press.

Straussner, S., Weinstein, D., & Hernandez, R. (1979, November). *Health and social work, 4*(4).

Streissguth, A. (1978). "Fetal alcohol syndrome." Paper presented at the Second Annual Alcohol Abuse Conference, University of California, Berkeley.

Student club shines light on drug abuse prevention. (1989, May 26). *Class Act*. Arlington, TX: Arlington Independent School District.

Swett, W. (1984, August). Helping young people survive in a chemical world. *Family and Community Health*, 63-73.

Technical Systems Institute. (1980, April 25). *Final report on drinking practices and alcohol-related problems of Spanish-speaking persons in three California locales*.

Tennes, K., Avitable, N., Blackard, C., Boyles, C., Hassoun, Holmes, L., Krye, M. (1985). Marijuana: Prenatal and postnatal exposure in the human. In T. Pinkert (Ed.), *Consequences of Maternal Drug Abuse* [Research Monograph], *59*, 48-60. Rockville, MD: National Institute of Drug Abuse.

Titmuss, R. (1968). *Commitment to welfare*. New York: Pantheon.

U.S. Department of Health and Human Services. (1987, November). PHS, ADAMA, *Literature review on alcohol and youth*. Rockville, MD: The National Clearinghouse for Alcohol and Drug Information.

U.S. Department of HEW, PHS, Marijuana and Health. (1980). Eighth Annual Report to the Congress from the Secretary of HEW, 1980 (DHEW Pub. No. ADM 80-945). Washington, DC: U.S. Government Print Office.

U.S. House of Representatives. (1984). Select Committee on Aging. *World Health Systems: Lessons for the United States*. Washington, DC.

Waddell, J., & Everett, M. (1980). *Drinking behavior among Southwestern Indians*. Tucson: University of Arizona Press.

Washington, V., & Oyemade, U. J. (1985, September). Changing family trends: Head Start must respond. *Young Children*.

Watts, T. (1982). Three traditions in social thought on alcoholism. *The International Journal of the Addictions*, *17*(7), 1231-1239.

Watts, T. D. (Ed.) (1986). *Social thought on alcoholism: A comprehensive review*. Malabar, FL: Krieger Publ. Co.

Watts, T. D., & Lewis, R. G. (1988). Alcoholism and native American youth: An overview. *Journal of Drug Issues*, *18*(1), 69-86. (Reprinted in *Akwesasne Notes*, 1988, Winter, *21*(1) 6-10.

Watts, T. D., & Wright, R., Jr. (Eds.) (1983). *Black alcoholism: Toward a comprehensive understanding*. Springfield, IL: Charles C Thomas Publ. Co. Also see R. Wright, Jr., & T. D. Watts (Eds.), *Prevention of Black Alcoholism: Issues and Strategies*. Springfield, IL: Charles C Thomas Publ., 1985; T. D. Watts & R. Wright, Jr. (Eds.), *Black Alcohol Abuse and Alcoholism: An Annotated Bibliography*. New York: Praeger Publ. Co., 1986; T. D. Watts & R. Wright, Jr. (Eds.), *Alcoholism in Minority Populations*. Springfield, IL: Charles C Thomas Publ., 1989; and R. Wright, Jr. and T. D. Watts (Eds.), *Alcohol Problems and Minority Youth*. Lewiston, NY: The Edwin Mellen Press, 1989; and T. D. Watts and R. Wright, Jr. (1988). Alcoholism and the Urban Black Population, *City Medicine: Current Concepts in Inner-City Health*, *2*(5), 4-7.

Wegscheider, S. (1980). *Another chance: Hope and health for the alcoholic family*. Pompano Beach, FL: Health Communications.

Weibel, J. C., & Weisner, T. (1980). The ethnography of urban and rural Indian drinking practices in California: Annual report to the Department of Alcohol and Drug Abuse Programs, Sacramento.

Weibel-Orlando, J. (1984). Substance abuse among American Indian youth: A continuing crisis. *Journal of Drug Issues*, *14*(2), 313-335. Also see: Weibel-Orlando, J. (1989). Treatment and prevention of Native American alcoholism. In T. D. Watts and

R. Wright, Jr. (Eds.), *Alcoholism in Minority Populations* (pp. 121-139). Springfield, IL: Charles C Thomas Publ.

Wheeler, W. (1977). *Counseling from a cultural perspective*. Atlanta, GA: A. L. Nellum and Associates.

Williams, M. (1985, Summer). Alcohol and ethnic minorities: Native Americans—An update. *Alcohol Health and Research World, 9*(4), 66-67.

Wilson, G., Desmond, M. M., & Wast, R. B. (1981). Follow-up of methadone treated and untreated narcotic-dependent women and their infants: Health, developmental and social implications. *J. Pediatr, 98*, 716.

Wilson, G., McCreary, R., Kean, J., & Baxter, J. (1980). The development of pre-school children of heroin addicted mothers; a controlled study. In T. Glynn (Ed.), *Drugs and the Family* (DHHS Publication No. ADM 81-1151). Rockville, MD: National Institute on Drug Abuse.

Wood, R. (1980). Urban alcoholism. In, J. Waddell & M. Everett (Eds.), *Drinking Behavior Among Southwestern Indians*, pp. 217-221. Tucson: University of Arizona Press.

Wright, E. J. (1981). "Counseling from a cultural perspective." Paper presented at an NIAAA Workshop. Rockville, MD: National Institute on Alcohol Abuse and Alcoholism.

Wright, R., Jr., Saleebey, D., Watts, T. D., Lecca, P. J. (1983). *Transcultural perspectives in the human services: Organizational issues and trends*. Springfield, IL: Charles C Thomas Publ.

Zigler, E., & Trickett, P. (1978, September). IQ, social competence, and evaluation of early childhood intervention programs. *American Psychologist*.

Zuckerman, B. (1985). Developmental consequences of maternal drug use during pregnancy. In T. Pinkert (Ed.), *Consequences of Maternal Drug Abuse* [Research Monograph], *59*, 48-60. Rockville, MD: National Institute of Drug Abuse.

Appendix

A SELECTED BIBLIOGRAPHY OF BIBLIOGRAPHIES ON SUBSTANCE ABUSE

This brief bibliography of bibliographies is not comprehensive. This listing, however, should be of assistance to the reader in doing research on substance abuse topics.

Abel, E.L., comp., 1982. *Alcohol and Reproduction: A Bibliography*. Westport, CT: Greenwood Press, 219 p.

Abel, E.L., comp., 1979. *A Comprehensive Guide to the Cannabis Literature*. Westport, CT: Greenwood Press, 699 p.

Abel, E.L., comp., 1983. *Drugs and Sex: A Bibliography*. Westport, CT: Greenwood Press, 129 p.

Abel, E. L., comp., 1985. *Fetal Alcohol Exposure and Effects: A Comprehensive Bibliography*. Westport, CT: Greenwood Press, 328 p.

Abel, E.L., 1986. *Fetal Alcohol Syndrome: An Annotated Bibliography*. New York: Praeger Publs., 172 p.

Abel, E.L., comp., 1984. *Lead and Reproduction: A Comprehensive Bibliography*. Westport, CT: Greenwood, Press, 118 p.

Abel, E.L., comp., 1983. *Narcotics and Reproduction: A Bibliography*. Westport, CT: Greenwood Press, 209 p.

Abel, E.L., comp., 1982. *Smoking and Reproduction: A Comprehensive Bibliography*. Westport, CT: Greenwood Press, 163 p.

Andrews, T. 1977. *A Bibliography of Drug Abuse, Including Alcohol and Tobacco*. Littleton, CO: Libraries Unlimited.

Andrews, T. 1981. *A Bibliography of Drug Abuse. Supplement, 1977-1980*. Littleton, CO: Libraries Unlimited.

Aquino, J. & Poliakoff, V., eds., 1975. *Health Education, Drugs and Alcohol: An Annotated Bibliography*. Washington: National Education Association.

Ashenbrenner, C. & Feldman, S. 1980. *Drugs, A Multimedia*

Sourcebook for Young Adults. New York: Neal/Schuman Publishers.

Bahr, H.M. 1970. *Disaffiliated Man: Essays and Bibliography on Skid Row, Vagrancy, and Outsiders*. Toronto: University of Toronto Press.

Barnes, G.M.; Abel, E.L.; Ernst, C.A.S.; comps., 1980. *Alcohol and the Elderly: A Comprehensive Bibliography*. Westport, CT: Greenwood Press, 138 p.

Barnes, G. M., & Augustino, D. K., comps. 1987. *Alcohol and the Family: A Comprehensive Bibliography*. Westport, CT: Greenwood Press, 461 p.

Barnes, G.M., & Brown, R. J. 1982. *Alcohol and Youth: A Comprehensive Bibliography*. Westport, CT: Greenwood, Press, 452 p.

Chalfant, H.P.; Roper, B.S.; & Rivera-Worley, C. comps., 1980. *Social and Behavioral Aspects of Female Alcoholism: An Annotated Bibliography*. Westport, CT: Greenwood Press, 145 p.

Drug Abuse Bibliography. Troy, NY: Whitston Pub. Co.

Dawkins, M.P. (1983). Policy issues. In T.D. Watts, & R. Wright, Jr. (Eds.), *Black Alcoholism: Toward a Comprehensive Understanding* (pp. 206-220). Springfield, IL: Charles C Thomas Publ.

Einstein, S. 1983. *The Drug User: Personality Issues, Factors, and Theories: An Annotated Bibliography*. New York: Plenum Press.

Friis, R., comp., 1979. *Stress and Substance Abuse: A Bibliography*. Irvine, CA: Human Behavior Research Group.

Goodman, E. (1989). Let us talk more of healing the wounded. *Fort Worth Star Telegram*, September 10, sect. 4, p. 3.

Heath, D.B. & Cooper, A.M. 1981. *Alcohol Use and World Cultures: A Comprehensive Bibliography of Anthropological Sources*. Toronto: Addiction Research Foundation.

Holleyhead, R. 1980. *A Bibliography on Ethyl Alcohol for Forensic Science and Medicine and the Law*. Harrogate, Eng.: Forensic Science Society; Edinburgh, Scotland: Scottish Academic Press.

Iiyami, P., Nishi, S.M., Johnson, B.D. 1976. *Drug Use and Abuse Among U.S. Minorities: An Annotated Bibliography*. New York: Praeger Publ.

Kelso, D.R. & Attneave, C.L., comps., 1981. *Bibliography of North American Indian Mental Health*. Prepared under the auspices of the White Cloud Center. Westport, CT: Greenwood Press, 411 p.

King, L.M. & Lopez, R.L. 1976. *Black Adolescent Alcoholism: Useful and Related Annotated References. 1945-1975.* Los Angeles, CA: UCLA Adolescent Drug Abuse Etiologies Project.

Klein, C.; Horton, D.M.; Kravitz, M.; comps., 1980. *Bibliographies in Criminal Justice.* Washington, DC: Dept. of Justice.

Lecca, P.J., et al. (1978) "Hispanic Mental Health." *Presidents Commission on Mental Health, Volume III.* Washington, DC: Superintendent of Documents.

Lecca, P.J., & McNeil, J. (1985). *Interdisciplinary team practice: Issues and trends.* New York: Praeger Press.

Lecca, P. J., Greenstein, T., & McNeil, J. (1988). *A profile of Mexican American health: Data from HHANES.* Arlington, TX: Health Services Research.

Lecca, P.J., & Munoz, E. (1988). *A profile of Puerto Ricans health status in U.S.: Data from HHANES.* HHS, DAA, Long Island University Press.

Lobb, Michael L. and Watts, Thomas D., eds., *Native American Youth and Alcohol: An Annotated Bibliography.* Westport, CT: Greenwood Press, 1989, 167 p.

Mail, P. & McDonald, D.R.; comps., 1980. *Tulapai to Tokay: A Bibliography of Alcohol Use and Abuse Among Native Americans of North America.* Foreword and literature review by Joy H. Leland and indexes by Sandra Norris. New Haven: HRAF Press.

Manson, S.M.; Dinges, N.G.; Grounds, L.M.; Kallgren, C.A.; comps., 1984. *Psychosocial Research on American Indian and Alaska Native Youth: An Indexed Guide to Recent Dissertations.* Westport, CT: Greenwood Press, 228 p.

Menditto, J. 1970. *Drugs of Addiction and Non-addiction, Their Use and Abuse: A Comprehensive Bibliography, 1960-1969.* Troy, NY, Whitston Pub. Co.

Messolonghites, L. 1979. *Multicultural Perspectives on Drug Abuse and Its Prevention: A Resource Book.* Rockville, MD: National Institute on Drug Abuse, 149 p.

Molina, C., Lecca, P.J., & Aguirre, M. (1991). *Latino health: America's growing challenge.* Washington, DC: American Public Health Association.

National Institute on Alcohol Abuse & Alcoholism. 1979. *Alcoholism Prevention: Guide to Resources and References*. Rockville, MD, 88 p.

National Institute on Alcohol Abuse & Alcoholism. 1980. *Health Insurance Bibliography*. Rockville, MD, 17 p.

National Institute on Alcohol Abuse & Alcoholism. 1980. *Occupational Alcoholism Programs Bibliography*. Rockville, MD, 42 p.

National Institute on Alcohol Abuse & Alcoholism. 1977. *Subject Area Bibliography on Alcohol and the Fetus*. Rockville, MD, 18 p.

National Institute on Drug Abuse. 1981. *Bibliography on Multicultural Drug Abuse Prevention Issues*. Rockville, MD, 64 p.

National Institute on Drug Abuse 1975. *The CNS Depressant Withdrawal Syndrome and Its Management—An Annotated Bibliography 1950-1973*. Rockville, MD, 55 p.

National Institute on Drug Abuse. 1975. *LSD Research—An Annotated Bibliography: 1972-1975*. Rockville, MD, 102 p.

National Institute on Drug Abuse. 1975. *Methadone and Pregnancy: An Annotated Guide to the Literature*. Rockville, MD, 31 p.

National Institute on Drug Abuse. 1975. *Polydrug Use: An Annotated Bibliography*. Rockville, MD, 35 p.

National Institute on Drug Abuse. 1975. *Women and Drugs: An Annotated Bibliography*. Rockville, MD, 62 p.

Phillips, J.E. and Wynne, R. D. 1974. *A Cocaine Bibliography: Nonannotated*. Rockville, MD: National Institute on Drug Abuse, 131 p.

Rutgers University, Center for Alcohol Studies, Information Services Division, 1981. *Recent Topics in Alcohol Studies*. Piscataway, NJ.

Rutgers University, Center of Alcohol Studies, Information Services Division. 1981. *Alcohol Studies: Retrospective Bibliographies*. Piscataway, NJ.

Sells, H.F., comp., 1967. *A Bibliography on Drug Dependence*. Fort Worth, TX: Texas Christian University Press, 137 p.

Treiman, B.R.; Street, P.B.; Shanks, P. 1976. *Blacks and Alcohol:*

A Selective Annotated Bibliography. Berkeley: Univ. of California, School of Public Health. 87 p.

Trotter II, R.T. & Chavira, J.A. 1977. *El Uso De Alcohol: A Resource Book for Spanish Speaking Communities.* Atlanta: Southern Area Alcohol Education and Training Program.

Watts, T.D. & Wright, R. Jr., eds., 1986. *Black Alcohol Abuse and Alcoholism: An Annotated Bibliography.* New York: Praeger Publ., 265 p.

Willer, Barry and Vokes, David. 1989. *Prevention of Chemical Dependency Among Native American Families and Youth: An Annotated Bibliography and Review.* Buffalo, NY: State University of New York at Buffalo, 32 p.

SUGGESTED READINGS

Abel, E.L., comp., 1985. *Dictionary of Alcohol Use and Abuse: Slang, Terms, and Terminology.* Westport, CT: Greenwood Press, 189 p.

Abel, E.L., 1984. *A Dictionary of Drug Abuse Terms and Terminology.* Westport, CT: Greenwood Press, 144 p.

Abel, E.L., 1982. *A Marijuana Dictionary: Words, Terms, Events, and Persons Relating to Cannabis.* Westport, CT: Greenwood Press, 136 p.

Austin, G.A.; Macari, M.A.; Lettieri, D.J. 1979. *Guide to the Drug Research Literature.* Rockville, MD: National Institute on Drug Abuse, 397 p.

Downard, W.L. 1980. *Dictionary of the History of the American Brewing and Distilling Industries.* Westport, CT: Greenwood Press, 268 p.

Keller, M., ed. 1966. *International Bibliography of Studies on Alcohol.* New Brunswick, NJ: Rutgers Center of Alcohol Studies.

Keller, M.; Efron, V.; Jellinek, E.M.; eds. 1965. *CAAAL Manual: A Guide to the Use of the Classified Abstract Archives of the Alcohol Literature.* New Brunswick, NJ: Rutgers Center of Alcohol Studies.

Lender, M.E. 1984. *Dictionary of American Temperance Biography: From Temperance Reform to Alcohol Research, the 1600s to the 1980s.* Westport, CT: Greenwood Press.

Marin, G., & Marin, B. V. 1991. *Research with Hispanic Populations*. Beverly Hills, CA: Sage Publs., 1991.

National Institute on Alcohol Abuse and Alcoholism. 1971. *First Special Report to the U.S. Congress on Alcohol and Health*. Rockville, MD, 121 p.

National Institute on Alcohol Abuse and Alcoholism. 1974. *Second Special Report to the U.S. Congress on Alcohol and Health*. Rockville, MD, 170 p.

National Institute on Alcohol Abuse and Alcoholism. 1978. *Third Special Report to the U.S. Congress on Alcohol and Health*. Rockville, MD, 98 p.

National Institute on Alcohol Abuse and Alcoholism. 1981. *Fourth Special Report to the U.S. Congress on Alcohol and Health*. Rockville, MD, 206 p.

National Institute on Alcohol Abuse and Alcoholism. 1984. *Fifth Special Report to the U.S. Congress on Alcohol and Health*. Rockville, MD, 146 p.

National Institute on Alcohol Abuse and Alcoholism. 1987. *Sixth Special Report to the U.S. Congress on Alcohol and Health*. Rockville, MD, 147 p.

National Institute on Alcohol Abuse and Alcoholism. 1990. *Seventh Special Report to the U.S. Congress on Alcohol and Health*. Rockville, MD.

National Institute on Drug Abuse. 1987. *Drug Abuse and Drug Abuse Research*. The Second Triennial Report to Congress from the Secretary, Department of Health and Human Services. Rockville, MD, 246 p.

National Institute on Drug Abuse. 1977. *Primary Prevention in Drug Abuse: An Annotated Guide to the Literature*. Rockville, MD, 205 p.

Nelson, J.E.; Wallenstein-Pearson, H.; Sayers, M.; Glynn, T.J.; eds. 1982. *Guide to Drug Abuse Research Terminology*. Rockville, MD: National Institute on Drug Abuse, 130 p.

Alabama

Alabama Dept. of Mental
Health
P.O. Box 3710
Montgomery, AL 36130

Alaska

Alaska Council
on Prevention
7521 Old Seward Highway,
Suite A
Anchorage, AK 99502

American Samoa

Alcohol and Drug Program
Department of Human
Resources
Government of American
Samoa
Pago Pago, AS 96799

Arizona

Office of Community
Behavioral Health
Arizona Dept. of Health
Services
400 N. 24th Street
Phoenix, AZ 85008

Arkansas

Office on Alcohol/Drug
Abuse Prevention
Department of Human
Services
400 Donaghey Plaza N.
P.O. Box 1437
7th & Main St.
Little Rock, AR 72203

California

CA Alcohol/Drug Programs
Dept.
111 Capitol Mall
Sacramento, CA 95814

Division of Drug Programs
111 Capitol Mall
Sacramento, CA 95814

Colorado

Alcohol and Drug Abuse
Division
Dept. of Health
4210 East 11th Avenue
Denver, CO 80220

Connecticut

Connecticut Alcohol
and Drug Abuse
Commission
999 Asylum Avenue
Hartford, CT 06105

From: National Institute on Drug Abuse and the National Institute on Alcohol Abuse and Alcoholism. *National Directory of Drug Abuse and Alcoholism Treatment and Prevention Programs*. Rockville, Maryland, 1989, pp. xi-xiii. (Reprinted, with some omissions.)

Delaware
Bureau of Alcoholism
& Drug Abuse
1901 N. DuPont Highway
New Castle, DE 19702

District of Columbia
Office of Health Planning
& Development
Commission of Public
Health
425 "I" Street, NW.,
Room 3200
Washington, DC 20004

Florida
Human Services Program
18328 Crawley Road
Odessa, FL 33556

Georgia
Alcohol & Drug Abuse
Services
Division of Mental
Health/Retardation
Room 319
878 Peachtree St., NE
Atlanta, GA 30309

Guam
Comm. Support Services
Dept. of Mental Health
& Substance Abuse
P.O. Box 8896
Tamuning, Guam 96911

Hawaii
Office of Primary
Prevention-ADAB
P.O. Box 3378
Honolulu, HI 96801

Idaho
Bureau of Substance Abuse
Department of Health
& Welfare
450 West State Street
Boise, ID 83720

Illinois
State of Illinois Center,
IDA SA
100 West Randolph Street
Suite 5-600
Chicago, IL 60601

Indiana
Prevention and Planning
Department of Mental
Health
117 E. Washington Street
Indianapolis, IN 46204

Iowa
Bureau of Prevention
and Training
Iowa Division of Substance
Abuse
321 East 12th Street
Des Moines, IA
50319-0075

Kansas
SRS Alcohol and Drug
Abuse Svcs.
300 Southwest Oakley
Topeka, KS 66606

Kentucky
Substance Abuse Branch
Dept. for Health Services
275 East Main St.
Frankfort, KY 40621

Louisiana
Office of Prevention
& Recovery from
Alcohol and Drug Abuse
2744-8 Woodale Blvd.
Baton Rouge, LA 70805

Maine
Ofc. of Alc. & Drug Abuse
Prevention
Dept. of Human Services
State House Station #11
Augusta, ME 04333

Marlanas/Trust Territories
Health Services
Office of the Governor
Saipan, CM 96950

Maryland
Alcohol & Drug Abuse
Prevention Unit Dept.
of Health & Mental
Hygiene
210 W. Preston St.,
4th Floor
Baltimore, MD 21201

Massachusetts
Coordinator of Prevention
Division of Alcohol
and Drug Rehabilitation
150 Tremont Street
Boston, MA 02111

Michigan
Ofc. of Substance Abuse
Services
Dept. of Public Health
P.O. Box 30035
3500 N. Logan Street
Lansing, MI 48909

Minnesota
Chemical Dependency
Program Division
Dept. of Human Services
Space Center Building
6th Floor
444 Lafayette Road
St. Paul, MN 55101

Mississippi
Division of Alcohol
and Drug Abuse
Dept. of Mental Health
1102 Robert E. Lee Bldg.
Jackson, MS 39201

Missouri
Div. of Alcohol and Drug
Abuse
1915 Southridge
P.O. Box 687
Jefferson City, MO 65102

Montana
State of Montana
Alcohol and Drug Abuse
Division
1539 11th Avenue
Helena, MT 59620

Nebraska
Division on Alcohol
and Drug Abuse
NE Dept. of Public
Institutions
P.O. Box 94728
Lincoln, NE 68509

Nevada
Bureau of Alcohol
and Drug Abuse
505 East King Street,
Rm. 500
Capitol Complex
Carson City, NV 89710

New Hampshire
Office of Alcohol and Drug
Abuse Prevention
Health and Human
Services
6 Hazen Drive
Concord, NH 03301-6525

New Jersey
Prevention & Ed. Unit
NJ Div. of Alcoholism
129 East Hanover Street
Trenton, NJ 08608

New Jersey State Dept.
of Health
Div. of Narcotic & Drug
Abuse Control,
CN-360-RM. 100
Trenton, NJ 08625-0360

New Mexico
Substance Abuse Bureau
Crown Building
P.O. Box 968
Santa Fe, NM 87504-0968

New York
NY Division of Alcoholism
and Alcohol Abuse
194 Washington Avenue
Albany, NY 12210

Substance Abuse
Prevention
Executive Park S.
Albany, NY 12203

North Carolina
Division of Mental
Health/Mental
Retardation/Substance
Abuse Services
325 N. Salisbury Street
Albemarle Bldg.
Suite 1122
Raleigh, NC 27611

North Dakota
Division of Alcohol
and Drug Abuse
State of North Dakota
State Capitol
Bismarck, ND 58505

Ohio

Bureau on Alc. Abuse
and Alc. Rec.
Dept. of Health
170 North High Street
3rd Floor
Columbus, OH 43266-0586

State Prevention
Coordinator
Bureau of Drug Abuse
170 N. High Street
3rd Floor
Columbus, OH 43266-0586

Oklahoma

Department of Mental
Health
1200 N.E. 13th Street
Oklahoma City, OK 73105

Oregon

Prevention/Intervention
Coord.
Ofc. of Alc. & Drug Abuse
Programs
301 Public Service Building
Salem, OR 97310

Pennsylvania

Div. of Training
and Prevention
Ofc. of Drug and Alcohol
Programs
P.O. Box 90, Dept.
of Health
Health and Welfare Bldg.,
Room 929
Harrisburg, PA 17108

Puerto Rico

Dept. of Addiction Services
P.O. Box B-Y
Rio Piedras Station
Rio Piedras, PR 00928

Rhode Island

Dept. of Mental Health,
Mental Retardation
& Hospitals
Division of Substance
Abuse
Substance Abuse
Administration Building
Cranston, RI 02920

South Carolina

South Carolina Commission
on Alcohol and Drug
Abuse
3700 Forest Drive
Columbia, SC 29204

South Dakota

Division of Alcohol & Drug
Abuse
Joe Foss Building
523 E. Capitol St.
Pierre, SD 57501

Tennessee

Div. of Alcohol and Drug
Abuse
Dept. of Mental Health
Doctor's Building
706 Church Street
Nashville, TN 37219

Texas
Texas Comm. on Alcohol
& Drug Abuse
1705 Guadalupe St.
Austin, TX 78701-1214

Utah
Alcohol and Drug Abuse
Clinic
50 N. Medical Drive
P.O. Box 2500
Salt Lake City, UT 84132

Vermont
Office of Alcohol & Drug
Abuse Programs
103 S. Main Street
Waterbury, VT 05676

Virginia
Prevention, Promotion
& Library
Dept. of Mental Health,
Mental Retardation
& Substance Abuse Svc.
P.O. Box 1797
Richmond, VA 23214

Virgin Islands
Department of Health
Division of Mental Health
Alcoholism and Drug
Dependency
P.O. Box 520,
Christiansted
St. Croix, VI 00820

Washington
Bureau of Alcohol
& Substance Abuse
MAILSTOP, OB-44W
Olympia, WA 98504

West Virginia
Div. on Alcoholism & Drug
Abuse
West Virginia Dept.
of Health
1800 Washington St., East
Charleston, WV 25305

Wisconsin
Office of Alcohol & Other
Drug Abuse
Bureau of Community
Programs
1 West Wilson Street,
Room 434
P.O. Box 7851
Madison, WI 53707

Wyoming
Substance Abuse Programs
Dept. of Health & Social
Svcs.
Hathaway Bldg., Rm. 362
Cheyenne, WY 82002

Alabama
Division of Mental Illness
and Substance Abuse
Community Programs
Department of Mental
Health
200 Interstate Park Drive
P.O. Box 3710
Montgomery 36193

Alaska
Office of Alcoholism and
Drug Abuse
Department of Health
& Social Services
Pouch H-05-F
Juneau 99811

Arizona
Office of Community
Behavioral Health
Arizona Department
of Health Services
701 East Jefferson,
Suite 400A
Phoenix 85034

Arkansas
Office on Alcohol/Drug
Abuse Prevention
Donaghey Plaza, North,
Suite 400
P.O. Box 1437
Little Rock 72203-1437

California
Department of Alcohol
and Drug Programs
111 Capitol Mall, Suite 450
Sacramento 95814

Colorado
Alcohol and Drug Abuse
Division
Department of Health
4210 East 11th Avenue
Denver 80220

Connecticut
Connecticut Alcohol
and Drug Abuse
Commission
999 Asylum Avenue
3rd Floor
Hartford 06105

From: National Institute on Drug Abuse and the National Institute on Alcohol Abuse and Alcoholism. *National Directory of Drug Abuse and Alcoholism Treatment and Prevention Programs*. Rockville, Maryland, 1989, pp. xv-xvii. (Reprinted, with some omissions.)

Delaware
Delaware Division
of Alcoholism, Drug
Abuse and Mental Health
1901 N. DuPont Highway
Newcastle 19720

District of Columbia
Health Planning
and Development
1875 Connecticut Avenue,
N.W.
Suite 836
Washington, DC 20009

Florida
Alcohol and Drug Abuse
Program
Department of Health
and Rehabilitative
Services
1317 Winewood Boulevard
Tallahassee 32301

Georgia
Alcohol & Drug Services
Section
878 Peachtree St., NE.,
Suite 318
Atlanta 30309

Hawaii
Alcohol and Drug Abuse
Branch
Department of Health
P.O. Box 3378
Honolulu 96801

Idaho
Bureau of Substance Abuse
and Social Services
450 West State Street
7th Floor
Boise 83720

Illinois
Illinois Department
of Alcoholism
and Substance Abuse
100 West Randolph Street
Suite 5-600
Chicago 60601

Indiana
Division of Addiction
Services
Department of Mental
Health
117 E. Washington Street
Indianapolis 46204

Iowa
Iowa Department of Public
Health
Division of Substance
Abuse and Health
Promotion
Lucas State Office Building
4th Floor
Des Moines 50319

Kansas
Alcohol and Drug Abuse
Services
2700 West Sixth Street
Biddle Building
Topeka 66606-1861

Kentucky
Division of Substance
    Abuse
Department for MH-MR
    Services
275 East Main St.
Frankfort 40621

Louisiana
Office of Prevention
    & Recovery from
    Alcohol and Drug Abuse
2744-B Woodale Blvd.
Baton Rouge 70805

Maine
Office of Alcoholism
    and Drug Abuse
    Prevention
Bureau of Rehabilitation
State House Station #11
Augusta 04333

Maryland
Maryland State Drug Abuse
    Administration
210 W. Preston St.
Baltimore, MD 21201

Massachusetts
Division of Substance
    Abuse Services
150 Tremont Street
Boston 02111

Michigan
Office of Substance Abuse
    Services
Department of Public
    Health
3423 North Logan Street
Lansing 48909

Minnesota
Chemical Dependency
    Program Division
Dept. of Human Services
444 Lafayette Road
St. Paul, MN 55155-3823

Mississippi
Division of Alcohol
    and Drug Abuse
Department of Mental
    Health
Robert E. Lee State Office
    Building
11th Floor
Jackson 39201

Missouri
Division of Alcohol
    and Drug Abuse
Department of Mental
    Health
1915 South Ridge Drive
P.O. Box 687
Jefferson City 65102

Montana
Alcohol and Drug Abuse
  Division
State of Montana
Department of Institutions
Helena, MT 59601

Nebraska
Division of Alcohol
  and Drug Abuse
Department of Public
  Institutions
P.O. Box 94728
Lincoln 68509

Nevada
Bureau of Alcohol
  and Drug Abuse
Department of Human
  Resources
505 East King Street
Carson City 89710

New Hampshire
Office of Alcohol and Drug
  Abuse Prevention
Health and Welfare
  Building
Hazen Drive
Concord 03301

New Jersey
New Jersey Division
  of Alcoholism
129 East Hanover Street
Trenton 08625

Division of Narcotic
  and Drug Abuse Control
129 East Hanover Street
Trenton 08625

New Mexico
Substance Abuse Bureau
Behavioral Health Services
  Division
P.O. Box 968
Santa Fe 87504-0968

New York
New York Division
  of Alcoholism and
  Alcohol Abuse
194 Washington Avenue
Albany 12210

Division of Substance
  Abuse Services
Executive Park South, Box
  8200
Albany 12203

North Carolina
Alcohol and Drug Abuse
  Section
Division of Mental Health
  and Mental Retardation
  Services
325 North Salisbury Street
Raleigh 27611

North Dakota
Division of Alcoholism
  and Drug Abuse
North Dakota Department
  of Human Services
State Capitol/Judicial Wing
Bismarck 58505

Ohio

Bureau on Alcohol Abuse
  and Recovery
Ohio Department of Health
170 North High Street
3rd Floor
Columbus 43266-0586

Bureau of Drug Abuse
Ohio Department of Health
170 N. High Street
3rd Floor
Columbus 43266-0586

Oklahoma

Alcohol and Drug Programs
Oklahoma Department
  of Mental Health
P.O. Box 53277
  Capitol Station
Oklahoma City 73152

Oregon

Office of Alcohol and Drug
  Abuse Programs
301 Public Service Building
Salem 97310

Pennsylvania

Deputy Secretary for Drug
  and Alcohol Programs
Pennsylvania Department
  of Health
P.O. Box 90
Harrisburg 17108

Rhode Island

Rhode Island Division
  of Substance Abuse
Substance Abuse
  Administration Building
Cranston 02920

South Carolina

South Carolina Commission
  on Alcohol and Drug
  Abuse
3700 Forest Drive
Columbia 29204

South Dakota

Division of Alcohol
  & Drug Abuse
Joe Foss Building
523 East Capitol
Pierre 57501

Tennessee

Alcohol and Drug Abuse
  Services
Tennessee Department
  of Mental Health
  and Mental Retardation
706 Church Street
4th Floor
Nashville 37219

Texas

Texas Commission
  on Alcohol and Drug
  Abuse
1705 Guadalupe Street
Austin 78701-1214

Utah
Division of Substance
  Abuse
120 N. 200 West, 4th Floor
P.O. Box 45500
Salt Lake City 84145-0500

Vermont
Office of Alcohol
  & Drug Abuse Programs
103 South Maine Street
Waterbury 05676

Virginia
Office of Substance Abuse
  Services
State Department of Mental
  Health and Mental
  Retardation
P.O. Box 1797
109 Governor Street
Richmond 23214

Washington
Bureau of Alcohol
  & Substance Abuse
Washington Department
  of Social and Health
  Services
Mail Stop OB-44W
Olympia 98504

West Virginia
Division on Alcohol
  & Drug Abuse
State Capitol
1800 Washington St., East
  Room 451
Charleston 25305

Wisconsin
Office of Alcohol
  & Other Drug Abuse
1 West Wilson Street
P.O. Box 7851
Madison 53707

Wyoming
Alcohol and Drug Abuse
  Programs
Hathaway Building
Cheyenne 82002

Guam
Department of Mental
  Health and Substance
  Abuse
P.O. Box 9400
Tamuning 96911

Puerto Rico
Department
  of Anti-Addiction
  Services
Box B-Y, Rio Piedras
  Station
Rio Piedras 00928

Virgin Islands
  Division of Mental Health
    Alcoholism and Drug
    Dependency
  P.O. Box 520
  St. Croix 00820

American Samoa
  Social Services Division
  Alcohol and Drug Program
  Government of American
    Samoa
  Pago Pago 96799

  Public Health Services

  LBJ Tropical Medical Center
  Pago Pago 96799

Trust Territories
  Health Services
  Offices of the High
    Commissioner
  Saipan 96950

Index